A Century of
JAYHAWK

by Blair Kerkhoff

Foreword by Jacque Vaughn

TRIUMPHS

The **100** GREATEST VICTORIES in the HISTORY of KANSAS BASKETBALL

Bob Snodgrass
Publisher

Jeff Bollig
Editor

Brad Breon
Managing Editor

Darcie Kidson
Publicity

Randy Breeden
Art Direction/Design

Dust jacket design by Jerry Hirt

Select photos courtesy of University of Kansas Archives

Select photos courtesy of The Kansas City Star

Production Assistance: Michelle Washington, Sharon Snodgrass, David Power, Jeremy Styno, Gary Carson

Published by Addax Publishing Group, 8643 Hauser Drive, Suite 235, Lenexa, Kansas 66215

Printed and bound in the United States of America

DISTRIBUTED TO THE TRADE BY ANDREWS MCMEEL, 4520 MAIN STREET, KANSAS CITY, MISSOURI 64111-7701

ISBN: 1-886110-35-2

Library of Congress Cataloging-in-Publication Data

Kerkhoff, Blair, 1959-
    A century of Jayhawk triumphs : the 100 greatest victories in the
 history of Kansas basketball / by Blair Kerkhoff, Blair ; foreword
by Jacque Vaughn.
        p.   cm.
    ISBN 1-886110-35-2
            1. Kansas Jayhawks (Basketball team)—History. I. Title.
GV885.43.U52K47   1997
796.323'63'0978165—dc21   97-22743
                                                            CIP

This book is not an official publication of, nor is it endorsed by, the University of Kansas.

Dedication

To Mom and Dad, who took me to all the games I wanted to see.

"Phog" Allen in front of Allen Field House under construction.

Table of Contents

A Century of Jayhawk Triumphs

Acknowledgments

As I gathered information, it became clear that a book about Kansas basketball history cannot be written without the assistance of some folks who make information gathering their business.

The Kansas sports information department, headed by Doug Vance, again unlocked the file cabinets and blew the dust off of old photographs. Basketball contact Dean Buchan, who cannot leave his office for a workout without a dozen voice-mail messages awaiting his return, returned all of mine and could not have been more cooperative.

Barry Bunch and Ned Kehde at KU's Spencer Research Library amicably responded to countless requests for photographs. Nearly every black and white photo came from the library and sports information department.

Jeff Bollig was the best possible editor. He attended Kansas, served as a sports information director there and knows just about everything there is to know about sports in the state. His contributions extended beyond fixing copy. His knowledge of KU hoops, especially the Ted Owens and Larry Brown years, are reflected in many of the top-game choices for those periods.

After a Kansas seniors barnstorming game in April, Jacque Vaughn agreed to write the foreword. Where he couldn't really help was in selecting the games that were most meaningful to him. "There are so many for several reasons," he said. When we listed the games selected for the book that he participated in, Vaughn couldn't disagree. His only request: include the UCLA games. We agreed.

Many thanks to *The Kansas City Star*, which supported the book in its advertising columns, and to executive deputy managing editor Dinn Mann for supporting the idea. Thanks to Star photographer Rich Sugg for providing Senior Day shots.

Under the direction of Bob Snodgrass, Addax Publishing is doing terrific things in its sports books division. Snodgrass guided this book through its infancy then handed it to Brad Breon, who oversaw its completion with patience and courtesy. The artistic handiwork of Randy Breeden is evident on every page.

Finally, any project I undertake becomes a family affair and mine is the easiest to work with. Karen and the kids, Nate, Ben and Anna supplied the love and support. They make everything worthwhile.

Jacque Vaughn

There were so many great victories during my Kansas career, it's tough to single out a few. The best way to do this, at least for the home games, is to remember when I thought the field house was at its loudest.

The first one came during my freshman year against Indiana. We beat one of the great programs and I had the opportunity to win it with a three-point shot. The funny thing is, it wasn't supposed to end with that play.

The game was tied. The play was meant for Steve Woodberry, but they had overplayed him. He cut back door, but I didn't think I was going to be able to get the ball to him. The one thing I wasn't going to do was turn the ball over in that situation. At least we could go into another overtime.

I was on the right wing. I took a little in and out dribble and gave a little pump fake because I was looking to draw the foul. But the defender didn't want to jump into me, so he only put his hands up. That gave me the opening to pull up and shoot the three. Luckily, it went in. I had only played about 10 games and I was still trying to get comfort-able as a college player. That game helped immeasurably.

The other game I would single out is UCLA my junior year. We got so far behind in the first half. They came out and played remarkable. They were more athletic than teams we were used to. Tipped dunks, flying through the lane. We were kind of caught off guard. We had one of those halftimes where we regrouped and came out strong in the second half.

That was probably the most fun I ever had in a game. To look in their eyes and see the transition from 'We just blew you guys out' to 'I can't believe we're losing.' Plus, I grew up in Los Angeles with these guys. Toby Bailey, Charles O'Bannon. Guys I've known since the sixth grade. That made it special. I also remember making a spin move, maybe my favorite play in four years at Kansas.

I'm glad to see those games included in the book. Many of the victories that I took part in were good assist games for me, and that's what I'll take from Kansas. If I was going to leave a mark I wanted it to be my assists. My goal was to become the third 1,000-1,000 player, assists and points (along with Duke's Bobby Hurley and North Carolina

State's Chris Corchani) in NCAA history. When I injured my wrist and missed 10 games I knew I wasn't going to make it. But I finished with more than 800 assists, and there are a lot of great point guards in the NBA who didn't get 600 in their career.

Many people asked me after I got hurt if I regretted not applying for the NBA draft after my junior year. The answer is no. Coming back for my senior year gave me another year of childhood, and you can't put a price tag on that. It also gave me another year of maturity. I got a chance to laugh, joke around with teammates, do all the things college players do. At the same time, I felt disappointment because of the injury and the way our season ended. But I wouldn't have traded my senior year for anything.

Now that it's over I'm looking forward to joining the Kansas family. You come to Kansas and see the fans wave the wheat at football games and hear them chant Rock Chalk. I got chills running through the tunnel into the field house and I'd look at the "Beware of the Phog" sign on the north end. But it's the people who make the difference. When I see guys like Paul Mokeski, Dave Magley, Mark Randall, Rex Walters come back and still feel like part of the program, that's what great tradition is. It's a family feeling that continues long after you're finished playing.

In a sense this book also ties us together because great games are part of the tradition. By reliving the greatest games, I think you'll get a good feeling about the history of Kansas basketball. I was thrilled to be a part of it.

Aren't all triumphs great?

A coach would say that. Some players might say that. Right after a game, it's the standard line. Those who watch the games know better.

A Century of Jayhawk Triumphs chronicles the basketball program's history through 100 of its greatest victories. There are 100 game stories individually wrapped up, beginning with the first triumph, weaving through the program's prosperous life. It concludes with a handful of victories from 1996-97, one of the greatest seasons in Kansas history.

The more difficult question is, "What makes a victory great?"

Every NCAA Tournament victory is great. But there are 56,

and not all are included here.

Every victory that clinched a league championship is great, but Kansas has won 44 of those in five conferences - Missouri Valley, Big Six, Big Seven, Big Eight and Big 12. Not all are here.

Every conference tournament victory is great, but if holiday tournaments are counted, there are 110 of those.

Every victory against a nationally ranked team is great, but in the 1990s alone there are 45 of those.

If you're from Kansas, every victory over Kansas State is great. If you're from Kansas City, every victory over Missouri is great. Combined, there are 299 of those.

Where some of these conditions come together, like the Jayhawks victory over Kansas State for the 1988 NCAA Midwest Regional championship, were easy calls. Games where nets were cut stood a good chance of making the cut. Games that prompted Kansas students to revel on Massachusetts Street into the wee morning hours were slam dunks. Others were more difficult.

A disproportionate number of games selected were played in the past two decades and no slight to the first 80 years was intended. Every attempt was made to find the greatest games from all eras. But, unfair as this may seem, recent games are more significant. The remarkable growth in interest, at Kansas and college basketball in general, has made them so. Today, every Kansas game, even the exhibitions, is televised. Allen Field House has been sold out for years.

And Kansas has had more success in the Larry Brown-Roy Williams period than at any time in the program's history. One national title, four Final Four appearances, and college basketball's best record in the 1990s have elevated Kansas to an elite status among today's powers. The bar has been raised so high that anything less than a Final Four appearance is considered a disappointment these days.

The 100 victories are presented in chronological order. We can't vouch for the quality of play in that 1899 victory over the Topeka YMCA, although with a coach named James Naismith you've got to believe the Jayhawks at least knew more about the rules than most. The first triumph starts the list.

Clearly, some triumphs are more important than others and a top 10 list is presented toward the back of the book. No. 1 -

the 1988 national championship game against Oklahoma - is no shock. You might be surprised at some of the other selections, however.

The painful memory chapter comes next. Kansas' 1,630 victories are more than all but Kentucky and North Carolina, but it also has lost 710 games. Some hurt Kansas fans more than others. Of the top 10 heart-breaking losses, two have come to the same school. It'll come to you if you think about it (hint: both losses came to the same coach 26 years apart).

Chapters are separated by the program's seven coaches. Technically, nine have coached Kansas, but one, Karl Schlademan, quit after one game in 1920 to devote his energies to track. Another, former Kansas star Howard Engleman, took over the team for the final 14 games of 1947 after Phog Allen was ordered by doctors to take a rest after suffering a concussion. Allen went to California, wrote a book and decided to take recruiting more seriously. The result was a class that produced the Jayhawks' 1952 NCAA championship.

Several Kansas followers offered input and every suggestion was considered. The final list was my call. Feel free to disagree and you'll be heard, but come with some evidence.

And, yes, we know Kansas isn't 100 yet. The century won't be completed until after the 1997-98 season. If Kansas wins the national championship this spring, we'll be happy to update the list.

James Naismith

James Naismith

9 seasons: 1889-1907   **Record: 55-60**

Kansas did not belong to a conference under Naismith

Home courts: Snow Hall basement (1898-1906)

               Roller skating rink at 807 Kentucky Street (1898-1901)

               Lawrence YMCA at 937 Massachusetts Street (1898-1902)

In a 1914 speech to the eighth annual NCAA Convention, Kansas physical education professor Dr. James Naismith said the ideal basketball player was "primarily a gentleman, secondarily a college man, and incidentally a basket ball player."

Naismith, basketball's inventor, might well have thought of himself as primarily a doctor, secondarily an educator and incidentally the Jayhawks' first basketball coach.

Kansas chancellor Francis Snow was looking for a physical education director and prayer leader for daily chapel in 1898 when he called his friend, University of Chicago chancellor William Harper. The message was relayed to Chicago football coach Amos Alonzo Stagg, Naismith's former coach at Springfield (Mass.) College.

Naismith was working at the Denver YMCA when he accepted Snow's offer, which said nothing about coaching basketball. It couldn't. Kansas didn't have a team.

Basketball had been played in Lawrence before Naismith's arrival - by women. But it didn't catch on. Football was the dominant sport of the day and the annual game with Missouri in Kansas City was the year's most important athletic event.

Naismith organized basketball at Kansas and interest grew rapidly. A tournament was held to select the first team, and on Feb. 3, 1899, Kansas played its first game in Kansas City, Mo., against the Kansas City YMCA. The Jayhawks lost 16-5.

But Kansas proved to be an able team. It won six straight after the loss, including a rematch with the Kansas City YMCA in Lawrence. The first Jayhawks team finished 7-4. There wouldn't be another winning season until 1905-06, when a freshman named Forrest C. Allen was the star player.

Kansas won its first game against another college, defeating neighboring Haskell 29-8 in 1899. In its first game against a future conference opponent, Kansas lost at Nebraska 48-8 in 1900. The outcome stands as the largest losing margin in Kansas history.

Naismith's career mark of 55-60 makes him the only coach in the program's history with a losing record. But Naismith didn't consider himself a coach. He officiated many of the games - that's mostly why he accompanied the team on the road. He usually didn't attend practices.

Naismith handed over the team to Allen in 1907. He remained in the physical education department at Kansas for the next three decades and died in 1939, two years before the Naismith Hall of Fame opened in Springfield.

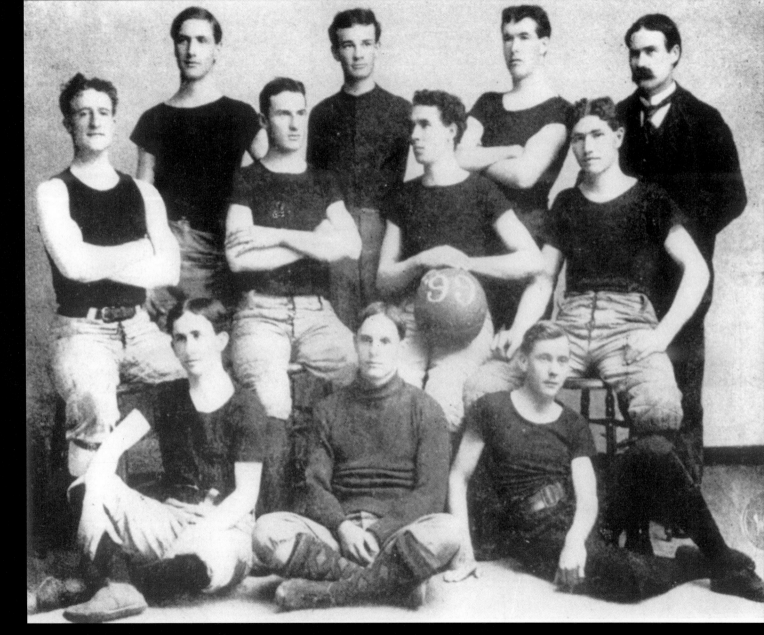

Kansas first team, 1898-1899.

First victory comes in second game
Feb. 10, 1899

Lawrence - Organized basketball would have started at Kansas at some point, but it was more than a happy coincidence that the game and its inventor arrived on campus about the same time.

In the late fall of 1898, Naismith arranged a school-wide tournament and the best players would make up Kansas' first team. Picking a team was fun, finding a place to play wasn't.

There was no campus gymnasium. The team was forced to use the basement of Snow Hall. The floor was 36 feet wide and 84 feet long, and the ceiling was 11 feet from the ground. A few years later, Naismith discovered space under the floor and had it dropped five feet, but the space remained inadequate, even by the day's standards.

Basketball was popular in athletic clubs and YMCAs, and those organizations provided most of the Jayhawks' early opponents. The first game by a Kansas team was played Feb. 3, 1899 in Kansas City, Mo., and the Jayhawks lost to the Kansas City YMCA 16-5. About 150 watched and Naismith, as he would for many Kansas road games, served as the referee.

A week later, Kansas played its second game. A team from the Topeka YMCA visited Snow Hall. It was no match for the Jayhawks, who won easily. The team's first star was William Sutton, the captain, who scored 13 points.

Kansas posted six more victories and finished 7-4 that season. Perhaps the most important games of the year were a pair of losses in late March to an Independence, Mo., YMCA team. The games were played in a barn and when they were completed, the Jayhawks presented a banner to the Independence players that said "championship of Missouri and Kansas."

Playing for the Independence team was Pete Allen, a terrific athlete who went on to become a three-sport letter winner at Kansas. Pete's younger brother, Forrest, was his biggest fan. Forrest would accompany Pete to athletic events, and he was in the hayloft for those two games against Kansas.

No telling what impression the games had on 14-year old Forrest Allen. But for the first time, he had watched a Kansas team in person, and young Forrest was beginning to develop some athletic skills of his own. Little did anyone know at the time but that fan in the hayloft would have the greatest influence on athletics at Kansas and become one of basketball's most remarkable figures.

Ted O'Leary on James Naismith

66 He came to all the games, sat on the second row in the middle of Hoch and hardly ever changed expression. He never applauded. He just watched the games. He really didn't give a damn about basketball. It was far more interesting to him to teach fencing to a small group and he was fascinated by wrestling. Basketball to him was of no great consequence. 99

James Naismith.

Phog breaks out
Feb. 12, 1906

Lawrence - In 1905-06, Kansas had two out-standing freshmen, Forrest C. "Phog" Allen and Tommy Johnson. They played for the first time Feb. 8 against the Wyandotte Athletic Club. Allen scored eight points on one field goal and six free throws.

The next day, the Jayhawks traveled to Allen's hometown and defeated the Independence Athletic Club 43-16. Allen scored 10. By now, Allen and Johnson were in the starting lineup.

Allen's breakout game came a few days later against Nebraska. The teams were playing for the first time in three years. The first score came five minutes into the contest on Allen's free throw. That got things rolling. When it was over, Allen had 23 on eight field goals and seven free throws, personally outscoring the Cornhuskers.

Allen wasn't finished. As Kansas rolled toward its most successful season, Allen saved his best for last. In a March 3 game against Emporia State, he scored 26 on 10 field goals and six free throws, a school scoring record that would stand until 1913.

Kansas finished 12-7, the most successful season under James Naismith and the only year that Allen played for the Jayhawks.

Forrest C. "Phog" Allen

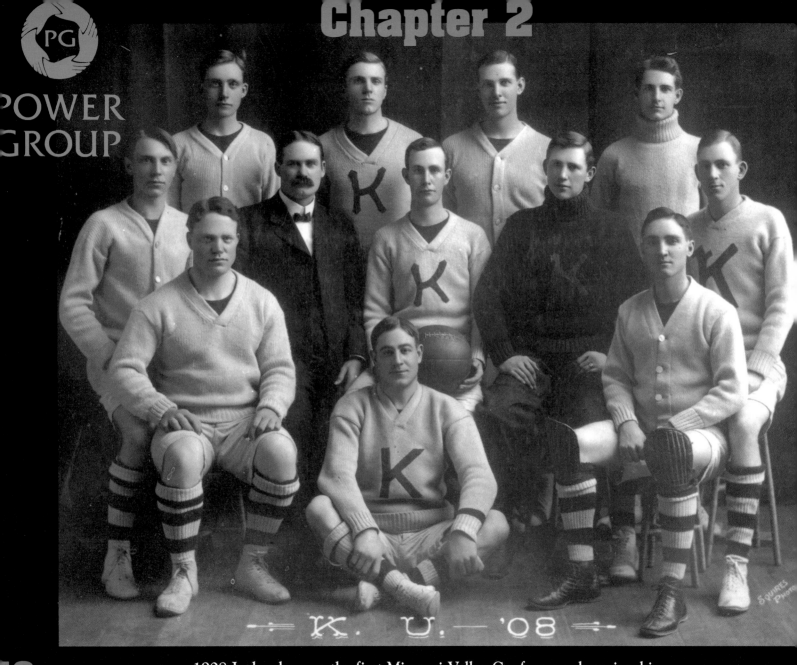

K. U. '08

1908 Jayhawks won the first Missouri Valley Conference championship.

Forrest "Phog" Allen
2 seasons: 1907-1909
Conference championships: 1908, 1909
Home court: Robinson Gym (3,000)

Record: 43-9

After one year as a KU student, Allen dropped out to find work. He became the football and basketball coach at his old school, Independence (Mo.) High, worked as a grocery store clerk and started his college coaching career at Baker in Baldwin City, Kan. Allen coached at Baker and Kansas in 1908 and at Haskell and Kansas in 1909.

Allen replaced Naismith and had two advantages over his predecessor: a conference and a new gym.

The Jayhawks along with Missouri, Nebraska, Iowa and Washington University of St. Louis formed the Missouri Valley Intercollegiate Athletic Association at a Jan. 12, 1907 meeting in Kansas City.

One reason Naismith stepped down was to oversee the construction of Robinson Gym, which was designed to look like the Springfield, Mass., YMCA where Naismith invented the game.

With 1,500 lockers, a swimming pool and 3,000 seats for spectators, the $100,000 structure was magnificent by the day's standards. Kansas christened the new floor with a 66-22 victory over Ottawa University on Dec. 13, 1907.

Many more victories followed as Allen upgraded the program. None of the previous teams played more than 19 games in a season. Allen scheduled the Jayhawks for 24 his first year and 28 the second.

Kansas captured the first two Missouri Valley championships, defeating Nebraska for the title both times. Allen's first team owned a 12-game winning streak, and his second opened the season with 19 straight triumphs. The fast start stood as a school record until 1935-36.

Those seasons proved to Allen something Naismith never believed, that basketball could be coached. But to be even more successful, Allen knew he'd need more training. Not on the court but in the medical field. In a time before team trainers, Allen understood that a coach who could keep his players healthy would have a huge advantage.

So Allen stepped down at Kansas after the 1908-09 season and enrolled at Central College of Osteopathy in Kansas City. He received the only degree of his life two years later and was hired by Central Missouri State to take over the athletic program. Allen, now widely known as "Phog" remained in Warrensburg for seven years, his teams winning nearly every conference championship.

Robinson Gym was dedicated on Dec. 13, 1907, the day Phog Allen coached his first game for the Jayhawks.

Robinson Gym dedicated with victory
Dec. 13, 1907

Lawrence - Phog Allen had agreed to coach the Jayhawks only two days before the 1907 season opener, the dedication game of Robinson Gym. He was starting his third year as Baker's coach but couldn't pass up the chance to coach the school he attended.

It's natural to wonder if Allen attempted to be a player-coach that season. He often had played that role, and although he had been out of school for a year working various jobs, he had just turned 22 when he took the Jayhawks' job. If Allen had re-enrolled and played for another two years, there's no telling how it may have influenced his career.

But Allen as a young coach was just as enthusiastic as Allen the player. Kansas set scoring school records in his lone season as a player, and it did in his first year as a coach.

Ottawa University was typical of the day's regional opponents. It was close and small. The first decade of Kansas basketball is filled with schools that today are classified as NAIA or NCAA Division II or III - William Jewell, Emporia State, Washburn, Baker, Bethany and Ottawa. YMCAs and city athletic clubs also were regular opponents in the days before conference affiliation.

Little is known about the victory over Ottawa, except the 66 points were the most ever scored by a Kansas team and atypical of scores of the day. The Jayhawks won 18 games in 1907-08 and scored more than 40 in three of them.

If game accounts are accurate, Kansas scored the contest's first 31 points.

First conference title goes to Kansas
Feb. 22, 1908

Lincoln, Neb. - Getting a conference up and running is a tricky thing today. Imagine the difficulty when the concept of a conference was new.

The Missouri Valley was formed in January, 1907 with five schools, but when the first conference basketball season opened in 1907-08, Drake had joined. That allowed the league to split into divisions with Kansas, Missouri and Washington of St. Louis, in the South and Nebraska, Iowa State and Drake in the North.

Only games against division teams counted in the standings. The problem was, Nebraska didn't face Iowa State or Drake that year. Washington, Drake and Iowa State all played only one game within the division.

The championship was determined by matching teams with the best overall records and in 1908 that was Kansas and Nebraska. It just so happened those teams were scheduled to meet in the final two games of the season in Lincoln. The series would determine the league title. If they split a third game would be played.

Nebraska had already defeated Kansas twice in Lawrence, and the Jayhawks were playing their eighth game in nine days - all on the road. Kansas had won all but one, to the Des Moines YMCA, and were on a roll.

The success continued in Lincoln. KU took the opener 28-26. The next day, the Jayhawks captured the first Missouri Valley championship with a 28-25 victory. The games, as the scores indicated, were similar. Neither side had a big lead and no one player stood out for Kansas.

William Hamilton

William O. Hamilton

10 seasons: 1910-1919   **Record: 123-59**
Conference championships: 1910, 1911, 1912, 1914, 1915
Homecourt: Robinson Gym (3,000)

William O. Hamilton had been a coach at Central High in Kansas City from 1902-1909. Before then, he coached basketball and ran the physical education department at William Jewell College in Liberty, Mo. Kansas wasn't getting a novice.

Phog Allen started the Jayhawks' winning tradition, building a 43-9 record over the previous two seasons. Hamilton's teams picked up where Allen left off.

The 1910 Jayhawks went 18-1, for a .947 winning percentage that remains a school record. The lone loss in Hamilton's first year was to Washington of St. Louis, a team Kansas defeated three other times that year, including a 46-7 decision in the season's third game. The team's stars were Vern "Shorty" Long, who led Kansas with 221 points, and Tommy Johnson.

Hamilton's teams followed with records of 12-6, 11-7, 16-6, 17-1 and 16-1. Kansas State was the only team to beat the Jayhawks in 1914 and 1915. In Hamilton's first six years, Kansas won or shared five Missouri Valley championships and went 23-1 against Missouri. The 1913 team was the first not to win a league title.

Hamilton differed from many coaches of his era by substituting freely. At a time when players needed to accumulate enough playing time to earn a letter, several of Hamilton's teams included nine or 10 letterwinners.

Ralph "Lefty" Sproull became the first player to lead the Missouri Valley in scoring for three straight years (1913-15). Sproull, a 6-3 forward, was considered the ideal athlete by James Naismith simply because of his physical measurements.

When the Sproull-era ended, so did Hamilton's success. His final four teams finished 35-37. League dominance passed to Nebraska and Kansas State, then to Missouri, which won four conference championships between 1918 and 1922.

Hamilton had also served as the Jayhawks' athletic director. He stepped down from both jobs after the 1919 season, ending 23 years as a coach, to devote more time to a budding Chevrolet dealership. He remained in Lawrence, a supporter of Kansas athletics until his death in 1951.

Hamilton's daughter, Mary, married Tusten Ackerman, a standout basketball player in the 1920s.

Ralph "Lefty" Sproull's 40 points in a 1913 game
stood as a school record until 1952.

Sproull goes for 40
Feb. 8, 1913

Lawrence - Ralph "Lefty" Sproull was the perfect physical specimen, symmetrically ideal according to James Naismith, who administered physicals to all incoming Kansas freshmen.

Sproull also was a terrific basketball player, the best to play for William Hamilton. As a three-year starter from 1913-15, the Jayhawks went 49-8 and won the Missouri Valley championship twice. Sproull led the league in scoring all three years, joining Ray Ebling (1934-36) and Clyde Lovellette (1950-52) as the only Jayhawks to pull off the triple.

Sproull's most amazing scoring feat came as a sophomore. In a home game against league foe Washington, he scored 40 points, a remarkable figure for the period. That season, Kansas scored fewer than 40 in 12 of 22 games.

Was Sproull ahead of his time? Yes and no. No doubt he was an exceptional athlete and that allowed him to take advantage of some peculiar rules of the day. Free throws not only were shot for fouls but also for violations like traveling and double dribbling. And one player could shoot all the team's free throws.

Against Washington, Sproull made all of Kansas' 12 free throws. He added 14 field goals.

The game didn't generate much publicity. As point totals for later Jayhawks started climbing into the the 20s and 30s, no mention was ever made of Sproull's effort. Lovellette actually broke the record with a 44-point effort against St. Louis in a 1952 NCAA Tournament game.

"I had scored 20 points the night before as we beat the same Washington U. team," Sproull said in 1968. "As we were warming up for the game, this little guard, Lacey was his name, came down and told me that he had been benched because I had scored too many points on him the night before.

"I asked him who was going to guard me and Lacey said the captain. I proceeded to have one of those nights when everything I threw in the general direction of the basket was on target. After the game, Lacey came to our dressing room and told me, 'Coach says I can have my job back.'"

1914 Jayhawks shared the Missouri Valley championship with Nebraska.
Coach William Hamilton stands next to captain Lefty Sproull on the second row.

Title is Hamilton's last
Jan. 22, 1915

Lawrence - The only champions in the first nine years of the Missouri Valley were Kansas and Nebraska. In six of the first seven years of the conference, the league was split into a South (Kansas, Missouri, Washington and, in 1914, Kansas State) and North (Nebraska, Iowa State and Drake).

From 1908-11 and in 1913, a season-ending playoff determined the champion. Kansas won the first three and the Cornhuskers broke through in 1911 and 1913.

Divisional play ended for the 1914-15 season, but the Jayhawks and Cornhuskers continued to be the class of the Missouri Valley. Their two games early in the season would determine the league champion.

Kansas looked to make an immediate statement. The game was particularly physical and a Nebraska player was tossed out for rough play. The Jayhawks got 14 points from Ephraim Sorensen and 10 from Lefty Sproull to rout the Cornhuskers.

The next day's game, also in Lawrence, was closer. But Kansas prevailed 30-23 to clearly establish itself as the premier team in the conference.

The Jayhawks finished with a 16-1 record, but it would be their last league title under William Hamilton.

Tigers' perfect season foiled
Feb. 21, 1918

Columbia - For the 1917-18 season, Missouri had hired as its coach Dr. Walter Meanwell from Wisconsin. He had won four Big Ten titles in six years and his first three Badgers teams compiled a 44-1 record.

Meanwell taught tight defense and disdained the dribble, preferring a short passing game. He brought this philosophy to the Missouri Valley and worked wonders with the Tigers, who made a strong bid for their first conference championship.

Not often in its history has Kansas played the spoiler, but that's the role the Jayhawks found themselves in when they traveled to Missouri. The undefeated Tigers trailed 13-7 at halftime.

Missouri closed to 20-16 but the Tigers couldn't keep Rudolf Uhrlaub off the line. He banged in 11 free throws to keep Kansas ahead.

The Tigers went on to their first conference title but Kansas kept them from an undefeated season. It would be William Hamilton's last significant victory. The Jayhawks finished 10-8, then 7-9 the next year before Hamilton resigned.

By the way, officials for the game were Phog Allen and Ernest Quigley, both former KU athletes and future athletic directors.

James Naismith and Phog Allen.

"Phog" Allen

37 seasons: 1919-1956

Record: 547-210
(590-219 in 39 seasons)

Conference championships: 1922, 1923, 1924, 1925, 1926, 1927, 1931, 1932, 1933, 1934, 1936, 1937, 1938, 1940, 1941, 1942, 1943, 1946, 1950, 1952, 1953, 1954.
National championships: 1922, 1923, 1952
Home courts: Robinson Gym (3,000) 1919-1929
Hoch Auditorium (3,000) 1929-1955
Allen Field House (17,200) 1955-
Note: The capacity of Allen Field House has changed over the years. Listed here is the capacity in the first year of a coach's tenure.

Allen was chosen over former football coach Bert Kennedy in 1919 to become the Jayhawks' athletic director. He had no intention of returning to coach. But four months into the job, basketball coach Karl Schlademan resigned after one game to devote his energies to track.

With no time to launch a coaching search, Allen appointed himself. He inherited some decent players, including all-around athletic star Dutch Lonborg. Kansas finished 11-7 and Allen decided to keep the job.

Good move. After one more so-so season, Kansas ripped off six straight conference championships and became the game's dominant force west of the Mississippi River. The 1922 and 1923 teams retroactively were named national champions by the Helms Foundation.

The Phog had rolled back in and Kansas was never the same.

In his second stint at Kansas, Allen won 22 league championships in 37 seasons. He had 62 all-conference selections, and 15 different players made at least one All-America team.

There wasn't a more accomplished coach in the game. In 1927, Allen was the driving force behind forming the National Association of Basketball Coaches. He vigorously fought for basketball's inclusion in the Olympic Games. He helped organize the first NCAA Tournament, and when the event bombed financially in 1939, Allen promised and delivered a successful event the next year in Kansas City.

Allen was a visionary. He and former KU football coach John Outland started the Kansas Relays, which grew into one of track and field's premier events. He inspired the construction of Memorial Stadium, one of

"Phog" Allen on motivation

❝A boy must say 'No' a thousand times to temptation before he can say 'Yes' once to victory.❞

29

Phog Allen has chalk talk with 1952 team.

the nation's oldest football arenas. In the 1940s, Allen blew the whistle on college basketball gamblers in New York, predicting the game's darkest hour.

When most coaches are retired, Allen won the biggest prize of all, the 1952 NCAA Tournament at age 66. Allen wanted to coach beyond the school's recommended retirement age of 70 and kicked up a public fuss when he was forced to step down.

Throughout his remarkable career, Allen touched the lives of many. Former players like Adolph Rupp and Dean Smith got their coaching foundations from Allen. Former squadman, U.S. Senator Bob Dole credited Allen with helping him through his near-fatal war wound. Jayhawk great Wilt Chamberlain wanted nothing more than to play for Allen.

To those who knew him only by reputation, Allen was a mythical figure, often called the most important man in Kansas. Perhaps. But we know for certain he was one of basketball's greatest coaches.

Bob Dole, in the Congressional Record, on Allen upon his death in 1974

"He convinced me there was more to life than football and basketball...and he helped me realize there could be other challenges and other rewards in my future. I shall always be in his debt."

Phog Allen portrait.

"Phog" Allen

1922 Missouri Valley co-champions. Captain George Rody holds the ball. Next to Phog Allen is Adolph Rupp, fourth from left. Paul Endacott is on the bottom row, second from left.

KU returns to title form
Feb. 21, 1922

Columbia - Kansas won the Missouri Valley in 1915 and then, by its standards, went into a deep sleep.

Nebraska, Kansas State and especially Missouri under coach Walter Meanwell became the new conference powers. From 1916 through 1921 the Jayhawks never finished higher than third or had fewer than seven league losses.

In 1922, the Missouri Valley was up to nine schools but Missouri remained the team to beat. The Tigers were rolling along, their undefeated record included a 10-point victory at Lawrence, their ninth straight over the Jayhawks. With the rematch in Columbia, Missouri seemed a cinch to win its third straight outright championship.

The Jayhawks were without starting forward Armin Woestermeyer, who found out at 5 p.m. on the day of the game that he had been ruled academically ineligible for the season's remaining four games.

Kansas led 12-10 at halftime and started to open the margin in the second half. Jayhawk forward George Rody, who did not make a shot in the first meeting, buried three second-half field goals on his way to a game-high 12 points. KU center "Long" John Wulf kept the Tigers away from the basket and Missouri finished with only five field goals. The Jayhawks had pulled the upset.

Kansas and Missouri won the rest of their games and both finished 15-1 in the Missouri Valley. A decade later, research by the Los Angeles-based Helms Foundation named the Jayhawks national champions for 1922 and guard Paul Endacott an All-America.

Phog's legend grows
Jan. 16, 1923

Columbia - Kansas shared the 1922 Missouri Valley championship with Missouri and had won at Columbia that season. But the Tigers had dominated the recent series, winning 21 of the previous 26 meetings with the Jayhawks.

Phog Allen knew his 1923 team could be fantastic. Players like Paul Endacott, Charlie Black, Tusten Ackerman and John Wulf were among the best in the conference. The Tigers, led by George Browning, Herb Bunker and future football coach Don Faurot, were also formidable. They were considered the league's best until somebody proved otherwise.

Kansas got that chance on Jan. 16 at Missouri's Rothwell Gym. Getting there was no easy task for the Jayhawks. They had played three games in three nights in Iowa from Jan. 11-13. After an overnight stay at Sedalia, the team got about nine miles from Columbia. But the train scheduled to bring the Jayhawks into town broke down. A truck arrived and got the team three miles from its destination before it broke down. The Kansas players and coaches covered the final distance on foot.

Rothwell was packed. Missouri took a 16-10 lead with about eight minutes remaining. Baskets by Endacott and Ackerman with three minutes left gave Kansas a late lead.

Then things got strange. In 1923, jump balls could be controlled by the jumper and there was no alternating possession. According to Allen, Endacott forced 16 jump balls in the final two minutes, stalling out the game and preserving the Kansas victory.

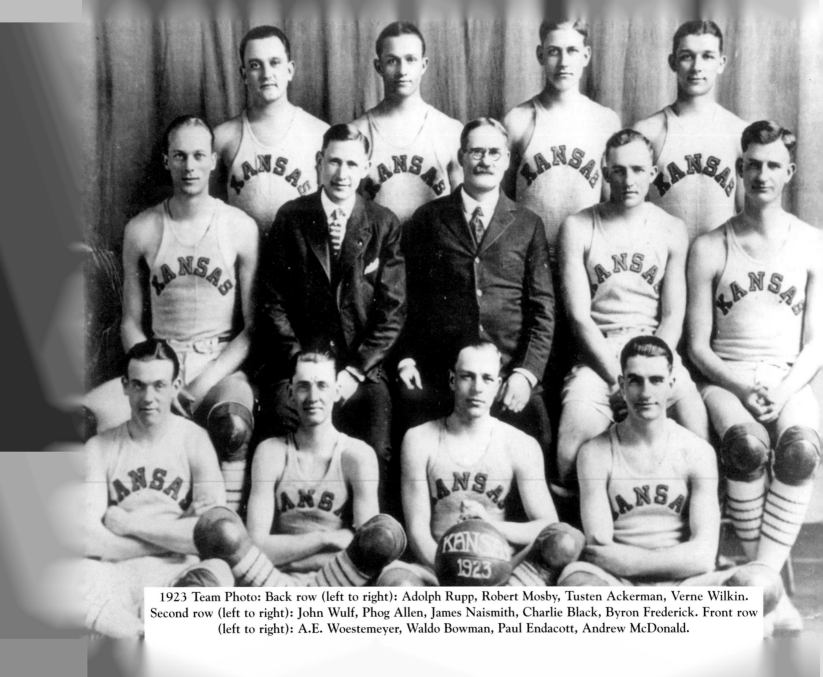

1923 Team Photo: Back row (left to right): Adolph Rupp, Robert Mosby, Tusten Ackerman, Verne Wilkin. Second row (left to right): John Wulf, Phog Allen, James Naismith, Charlie Black, Byron Frederick. Front row (left to right): A.E. Woestemeyer, Waldo Bowman, Paul Endacott, Andrew McDonald.

Phog's career saved
Feb. 28, 1923

Lawrence - Although the Jayhawks had defeated Missouri earlier in the season, Kansas had to win the regular season finale over the Tigers to win its first outright league championship since 1915.

Something greater was at stake: Phog Allen's career.

"Mrs. Allen told me in confidence that Phog had confided in her before the start of the 1923 season that unless he could win a clear-cut championship, which required that Missouri be defeated twice, he definitely would abandon coaching and thereafter engage only in Physical Education and Athletic Director activities," Paul Endacott wrote.

The Tigers were capable of winning. They had won 10 straight from KU in Lawrence heading into the Feb. 28, 1923 contest. It's the longest winning streak by an opponent at Lawrence in the program's 99 seasons.

Kansas started quickly and jumped to a 14-9 lead. Early in the second half, the lead grew to 18-10. But back came the Tigers. A free throw by George Browning cut the margin to 20-18.

With three minutes remaining, Tus Ackerman dropped in one of his seven free throws. Waldo Bowman followed with a basket to restore a five point lead. The Tigers scored in the final seconds for the three-point margin.

Allen called the season "ever victorious." The Jayhawks completed the year with a 16-0 conference record, which stands as Kansas' greatest league mark. The 1997 team finished 15-1 with only a double overtime loss at Missouri.

The season's lone loss came to the Kansas City Athletic Club, a non-conference game.

The 1923 season proved pivotal in the program's history. Kansas supplanted Missouri as the dominant program in the Missouri Valley. The Tigers had won or shared four of the previous five titles. Over the next 53 years, Missouri would win three more.

Allen and the Jayhawks were off and running. The 1923 championship was the second of six straight for Kansas, which wouldn't go more than three years between league titles until the late 1940s. The Helms Foundation named Kansas the national champion for the second straight year.

Members of the team remained close over the years, commemorating the season with five-year anniversaries that stopped in the 1970s.

36 How small was Hoch Auditorium, the Jayhawks' home from 1929-1955? It seated fewer than 3,000 for basketball. Notice how the corner meets the wall on the baseline.

Victory over Cats completes turnaround
Feb. 17, 1930

Lawrence - In 99 years of Kansas basketball, no season had been worse than 1929. The Jayhawks went 3-15 and finished tied for last in the Big Six for the first time.

Phog Allen vowed there would be no repeat the next season, and Kansas embarked on a remarkable turnaround. After 12 games of the 1929-30 season, the Jayhawks stood 12-0. The next opponent was Kansas State.

Kansas had defeated the Wildcats earlier in Manhattan, and 3,700 fans in Hoch Auditorium believed they could breathe easily when the Jayhawks took a two-point lead and the ball with 10 seconds left.

But KU's Frosty Cox committed a foul and the Wildcats went to the line for one free throw. The shot was deliberately missed, and two tap-in attempts hung on the rim before falling off. Kansas had its 13th consecutive victory.

The season peaked that night. The Jayhawks lost four of their next five, including two to Big Six champion Missouri. But the Jayhawks' 14-4 overall record represented the greatest one-year improvement in the program's three decades. The record would stand until the 1970s.

The 1930 campaign also marked the beginning of 18 straight winning seasons, the longest such streak in school history.

Midwest triumphs over East
Dec. 20, 1931

Kansas City - Until a three-game series against Pittsburgh at the Convention Center, Kansas had never played a team from the East, a part of the country that played inferior basketball, according to Phog Allen.

Now he had a chance to prove it. Pitt had one of the nation's top programs under coach Doc Carlson. The Panthers had been named national champions for 1928 and 1930 by the same organization - the Helms Foundation - that gave KU titles in 1922 and 1923.

The opening game was all Pittsburgh early. The Panthers led 17-11 at halftime and 21-13 early in the second half.

The Jayhawks scored six straight but fell behind 23-19 with four minutes remaining. Back came Kansas. Ted O'Leary's layup with two minutes left put the Jayhawks ahead 24-23. There was no more scoring, only furious play under both team's baskets. The Panthers got off several shots, but nothing fell, sealing the Kansas victory.

The Jayhawks won the second game 26-20. Pittsburgh took the third 25-22. Allen delighted in owning the series advantage. Allen and Carlson never again squared off, but that didn't stop Allen from continuing taking on Eastern comers. None came to Lawrence, so Allen took the Jayhawks there.

From 1940 until 1951, Kansas made four swings through the East, with Allen heralding the superiority of Midwestern basketball to city reporters at every stop.

Kansas and the rules

No school has had a more profound impact on college basketball's rules than Kansas, thanks mostly to Phog Allen and Wilt Chamberlain.

Allen was forever challenging the rulebook, attempting to shape the game to his idea. Mostly, Allen wanted guards to have more influence than the center. That's why he campaigned for 12-foot baskets throughout his career. Allen didn't want big men catching the ball in the lane for easy hoops and he hated the tip-in, believing it rewarded an offense for missing a shot.

A higher basket would allow rebounds to bounce out farther, eliminate congestion in the lane and thus reduce fouling.

Kansas kept a pair of 12-foot goals at its practice court in Robinson Gym. In 1934, the Jayhawks actually played two games with 12-foot hoops that count in the record book against Kansas State. The teams won on each other's home floor.

Allen never got the 12-foot basket but his outrage in 1927 against a proposal to eliminate dribbling was the inspiration behind the formation of the National Association of Basketball Coaches. Allen and other prominent coaches were outraged by joint decision by the AAU, NCAA and YMCA to end dribbling. More than 100 coaches met at the 1927 Drake Relays and even more in Chicago that summer to form the NABC. The group saved the dribble.

Allen also was successful in 1932. He believed there should be a 10-second rule for bringing the ball into the frontcourt. To prove his point, he ordered his team to keep the ball on the Jayhawks' end of the floor in a game against Missouri. Kansas was trailing 4-2 in the early moments when four players sat down and the fifth player stood with the ball on his hip. Four Tiger players sat down on their end of the floor and one stood in case the guy with the ball went to the basket. The next year, college basketball introduced a 10-second line.

Allen believed Chamberlain could make a mockery of the rules and would prove his theory of the 12-foot basket. Allen never got to coach Chamberlain, but the game's tallest player did change the rules. Because of him players could no longer leave the free-throw line immediately after releasing the ball. For Wilt, that was like passing it to himself. He used to tap in his many misses.

Goaltending rules also changed. Before the 1957-58 season it was legal to guide a teammate's shot into the basket. Offensive goaltending was banned.

Kansas 33, Oklahoma 29

Droning plane lands
Feb. 27, 1932

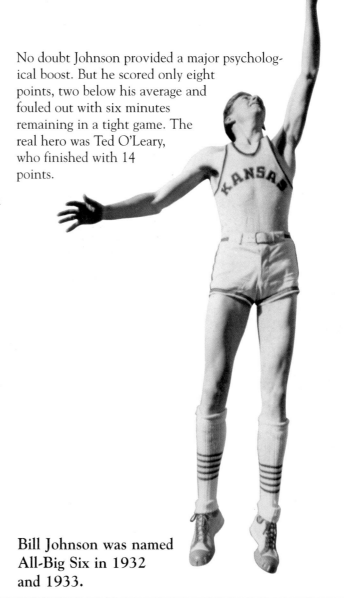

Lawrence - The Jayhawks and Oklahoma were tied for the Big Six lead heading into the season finale at Hoch Auditorium, and things looked bleak for Kansas.

Star center Bill Johnson wasn't expected to suit up. His father had died earlier in the week and the funeral in Oklahoma City was set for Saturday afternoon. Tip-off with the Sooners was scheduled for 7 p.m.

The Jayhawks had lost to Oklahoma in overtime at Norman earlier in the year, and Phog Allen believed they wouldn't stand a chance without Johnson. So he went to work.

Allen arranged to have Johnson flown from Oklahoma City late Saturday afternoon. He had contacted a friend there, Cobb Burnside, who hired a pilot - an Oklahoma grad it turned out - to fly Johnson to Lawrence.

Allen had told reporters that he didn't expect Johnson to play but when the players arrived to dress out, they knew something was up. Allen had moved the game time back to 7:30 p.m., telling the Sooners he wanted to give KU fans an opportunity to hear a radio broadcast of Kansas State-Missouri, a game that had bearing on the conference title race.

The flight left at 4 p.m. and landed in Ottawa more than two hours later. He arrived in Lawrence a little after 7 p.m.

The crowd of 3,500 roared their approval when Johnson took the floor. In later years, Allen made this game part of his story telling repertoire, with hand gestures and all, describing how in the lockerroom he cupped a hand to his ear and listened for the droning plane.

No doubt Johnson provided a major psychological boost. But he scored only eight points, two below his average and fouled out with six minutes remaining in a tight game. The real hero was Ted O'Leary, who finished with 14 points.

Bill Johnson was named All-Big Six in 1932 and 1933.

1936 Jayhawks huddle.

Phog wins a game and a son
Feb. 28, 1936

Lincoln, Neb. - Nebraska was seeking a share of its first Big Six championship and first conference title since 1916. A triumph over the Jayhawks would all but assure a co-championship with Kansas.

Practice the week of the game had been sluggish at Kansas, and Phog Allen wasn't happy with the play of his son, Milton ("Mitt"), the point guard. The two argued, which was overheard by some spectators. Phog Allen yanked his son and inserted Roy Holliday to run with the first team during workouts.

Phog Allen had Holliday ride with the first team to Lincoln while Mitt Allen rode in a car with the second team. The pregame storyline was would Mitt start? Phog Allen used it to his advantage.

Holliday started and the game was even most of the first half. Phog Allen knew his son, with wounded pride, would be motivated. Mitt was so keyed up, he fouled out during his abbreviated action. But not before leading the Jayhawks to the victory with superb leadership.

The game was close early, but after Allen was inserted, the Jayhawks soared to a 25-13 lead. The margin grew to 14 early in the second half. Nebraska got a record crowd of 7,000 excited by closing to six late, but the Jayhawks pulled away toward the end to guarantee the victory.

Ray Ebling finished with 16 points, with several baskets set up by Mitt Allen.

Mitt had always been something of a rebel. The incident not only helped Kansas win a Big Six championship and remain undefeated at 16-0, it went a long way toward bringing a father and son closer together.

Milton "Mitt" Allen in 1936, the first of two Phog Allen sons to play for the Jayhawks.

Pralle ends career with title
March 3, 1938

Lawrence - Basketball statistics started to become a little more sophisticated during the career of Ferdinand "Fred" Pralle.

When Pralle's career ended with a 22-point effort in a Big Six title triumph over Missouri, he was touted as one of the great players in Kansas history. Unlike previous great players, however, there were some numbers to support his case.

Pralle finished with 539 points in his three-year career. That total doesn't place him among the school's top 50 scorers today, but in 1938 they were solid numbers. Pralle led the Big Six in scoring as a senior with a 12.1 average. Then, only points scored in league games counted toward a scoring title.

We also know that Pralle started every game except one in three years and played every minute of all conference games except the final few ticks of games against Oklahoma and Missouri because he fouled out.

While several Kansas players had been named to an All-America team before 1938, Pralle became the Jayhawks' first consensus selection. He's one of seven to win such an honor, joining the likes of Clyde Lovellette, Wilt Chamberlain and Danny Manning.

Pralle saved one of his best games for last. His 22 against the Tigers delighting the Hoch Auditorium crowd that included James Naismith. At halftime, the first game was recreated by KU physical education majors. Nine on a side, playing a game that looked more like rugby.

But the night belonged to Pralle, who received a huge ovation when the game ended.

1938 Fred Pralle

1943 Charlie Black

1951-52 Clyde Lovellette

1941 Howard Engleman

1957-58 Wilt Chamberlain   1987-88 Danny Manning

1997 Raef LaFrentz

The Pony Express team of 1939-40.
From left John Kline, Dick Harp, Bob Allen, Howard Engleman, Ralph Miller.

KU has a ball with Aggies
March 16, 1940

Oklahoma City - The Jayhawks, who lost to Oklahoma in their last regular-season game, defeated the Sooners in a Big Six playoff game at Wichita to make the NCAA Tournament. Awaiting was Missouri Valley Conference champion Oklahoma A&M and the teams couldn't decided whose ball to use.

Kansas was still using a ball with laces. The Aggies were going with a seamless ball. Phog Allen and Hank Iba agreed to use the Jayhawks' ball in the first half and the Aggies' ball after that.

With the halftime score 24-24, Kansas had to feel like a loser at the break. But Oklahoma A&M fared no better in the second half, and despite playing with its ball, was probably at a greater disadvantage. The Aggies were playing their third game in four nights. They had just finished third at the NIT.

Neither side could gain an upper hand in the second half. The game was tied 40-40 for the final 1:30 of regulation.

A pair of Kansas free throws and a basket by the Aggies' Jess Renick made it 42-42 two minutes into overtime. Moments later Jayhawk guard Dick Harp made his only field goal of the game, an 18-foot swish.

Renick answered with a free throw, but that was it for Oklahoma A&M. KU All-America Howard Engleman dropped in a free throw with a minute remaining to end the scoring.

The game was only the 13th between the schools in what would develop into a fierce, but mostly friendly rivalry. And, as long as Allen and Iba were coaching, a methodical, patterned offense and defensive-oriented rivalry.

Kansas won the first seven meetings and the playoff triumph gave the Jayhawks a 10-3 series edge, but it wouldn't take long for Iba and the Aggies, NCAA Tournament winners in 1946 and 1947, to close the gap.

The 1940 Jayhawks reached the NCAA championship game. Back row (L-R): Herbert Hartman, James Arnold, John Kline, T.P. Hunter, Ralph Miller. Middle row (L-R): Trainer Dean Nesmith, Bruce Reid, John Krum, Bruce Voran, Bob Johnson, Bob Allen, head coach Phog Allen. Front row (L-R): Robert Woodward, Dick Harp, Don Ebling, Howard Engleman, Bill Hogben.

Engleman shoots KU to final
March 23, 1940

Kansas City - Sportswriters inspired the NCAA Tournament. Not for what they had written but for the money they were making off college basketball.

The Metropolitan Basketball Writers Association of New York ran the National Invitation Tournament, which sold out Madison Square Garden in the 1938 inaugural event.

Coaches believed money made on a tournament should go back to the schools. A National Association of Basketball Coaches group consisting of Phog Allen, ex-KU assistant John Bunn of Stanford and Harold Olsen of Ohio State were designated to work with the NCAA to come up with a postseason event.

The NCAA Tournament debuted in 1939 and was a financial bust. The Eastern championship was played in Philadelphia. The Western final was in San Francisco and the final on the campus of Northwestern in Evanston, Ill. Attendance was poor and the event ran a $2,531 deficit.

Allen promised the NABC and NCAA that if the tournament were brought to Kansas City, it would make money even if the Jayhawks didn't make the field.

But Allen didn't take a chance. He got Kansas to the Western final by knocking off Oklahoma A&M in a district playoff at Oklahoma City and Rice in a Western playoff in Kansas City behind Howard Engleman's 21 points.

Southern Cal was favored to beat the Jayhawks in the Western final. Allen got a scouting report from Bunn, who told Allen that the Trojans would try to force Kansas outside. The Jayhawks responded by knocking in one-handers from outside the free throw circle throughout the first half.

When Southern Cal challenged the Jayhawks outside, guard Dick Harp broke free for layups. The Trojans were off their game but capable of winning. They took a 42-41 lead with 1:30 to play on Jack Lippert's 20-footer, then got possession after a Kansas miss.

But KU's Bobby Allen left his man, created a double team on Lippert and stole the ball. The Jayhawks worked the ball around to Engleman, who dropped in a 12-footer from the side for the game-winner.

The championship game had sold out in advance, but with Kansas facing Indiana in the final, it became an even hotter ticket. When the tournament was over, the event had cleared nearly $10,000 and Allen had kept his promise.

Train trip inspires romp through East
Dec. 30, 1942

Philadelphia - Kansas opened the 1942-43 season with a loss to the Olathe Naval Air Base, coached by Jack Gardner. It eeked out a victory over Rockhurst (Mo.) College then lost the home opener to Creighton. A trip to the East loomed and Phog Allen didn't believe the Jayhawks possessed the proper spirit to win on the road.

Players and coaches shared a train to Buffalo, where the Jayhawks were to play St. Bonaventure, with World War II soldiers, some returning from battle. The players and soldiers mingled. When space was tight, players gave up their seats.

Allen believed the trip had a profound effect on the Jayhawks, who crushed the Bonnies 53-22. Two nights later, Kansas beat St. John's 31-30 at Madison Square Garden, then capped the trip with a 25-point triumph over St. Joseph's.

Allen could embellish stories with the best of them but seemed genuinely moved by his team's reaction to the soldiers. "Suddenly (the Jayhawks) discovered that there was much for them to be thankful for," Allen wrote in his book *Sports Stories*.

The road trip sparked a 12-game winning streak and created momentum for Big Six competition. Allen called the games and the trip a turning point in the season and it also may have served as an inspiration to the coach also.

A few months later, Allen started a publication, *Jayhawk Rebounds*, a monthly newsletter to players and alumni in the service. In it, Allen relived some of his favorite stories, updated the whereabouts of Kansas players, and provided news of KU athletes. It didn't take long for circulation to climb into the hundreds.

The trip made an impression.

"When our boys saw the such splendid morale and esprit de corps in our American soldiers and sailors then their petty differences faded away, and the big central theme was that if these service boys were willing to give their lives to their country, they can ride in chair cars without beefing or belly-aching, then unconsciously, I think, they thought it was up to us to do a bigger job," Allen wrote.

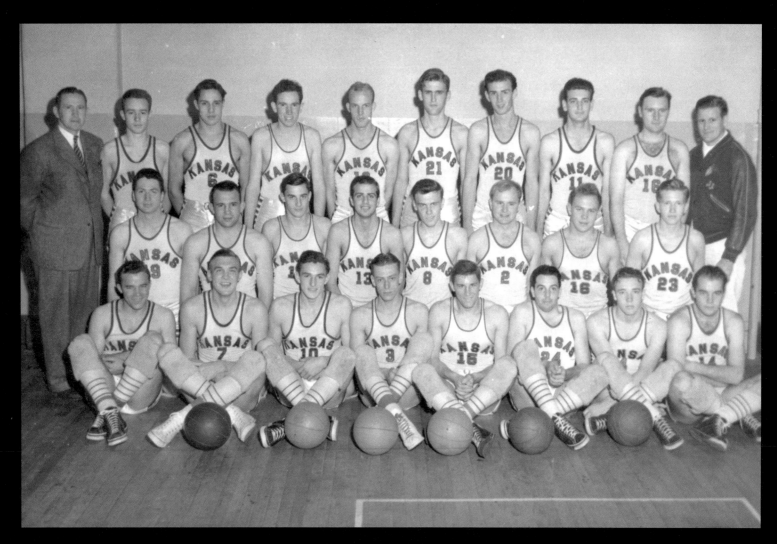

1942-43 team that went undefeated in Big Six competition. Third from the left on top row is Bob Dole.

A Century of Jayhawk Triumphs

A final crown before service
Feb. 26, 1943

Lawrence - A crowd of 3,384 packed Hoch Auditorium to see if the Jayhawks could wrap up the Big Six championship. It wouldn't be easy.

Second-place Oklahoma had given the Jayhawks all it could handle a month earlier when Kansas won by four at Norman. The Sooners had become a league power, sharing the championship with Kansas in 1940 and 1942, and they had the league's best player in Gerald Tucker.

And this time, the Jayhawks wouldn't be at full strength. Starters Charlie Black and Armond Dixon were out with injuries. This was Allen's "Iron Five" team, which also included John Buescher, Ray Evans and Otto Schnellbacher. The starters played nearly every minute.

But Kansas doesn't usually blow chances to win league championships on its home floor and the Jayhawks came out inspired. They led 15-11 at halftime in a defensive struggle. The lead stretched to 10 in the final few minutes, which were marked by emotional outbursts.

Evans played solid defense throughout the game and left to a standing ovation when he fouled out. With 10 seconds remaining, Kansas reserve Bill Brill and the Sooners' A.D. Roberts got in a fight at the scorer's table as they were preparing to check in to the game. Phog Allen and Sooners coach Bruce Drake quickly broke up the scrap.

With a handful of games remaining, the Jayhawks had their fourth straight conference title, and four of the starters - all but Dixon - made all-conference. But there would be no trip to the NCAA Tournament. Allen turned down the

Kansas scores against Oklahoma in the 1943 contest at Hoch Auditorium.

opportunity to participate in the district playoff because four starters were to be inducted into the service immediately after the regular season.

Allen had given those starters a weekend to spend with their families instead of playing in a game against powerful Creighton. Kansas suffered its most lopsided loss in five years, falling by 22.

But with the starters back, the Jayhawks completed a perfect (10-0) conference season by beating Kansas State to end the year. Oklahoma represented the Big Six in the NCAA Tournament, but the Jayhawks owned the conference trophy. Again.

Escape act keeps streak alive
Feb. 16, 1945

Manhattan - From 1938 to 1947, Kansas won 22 straight games against Kansas State. It's the longest such streak in KU history.

The streak appeared over at 17. The Jayhawks led 32-31 when Wildcats guard Dick Spencer took a pass from Dana Atkins and drove to the hoop for a layup. The crowd cheered loudly as the ball fell through the net.

Nobody had heard the whistle from referee Eddie Hogue. Atkins had been called for double dribble before Spencer got the ball. A last-second free throw by KU center Owen Peck completed the scoring.

Kansas State fans mobbed the floor. Wildcats coach Fritz Knorr, players and school military personnel escorted the officials from the building.

The Jayhawks didn't get away easily. Their car ties had been flattened.

A few days after the game, Phog Allen received a letter from a K-State fan that included a two-inch square from one of the official's shirts. Phog kept it hung up on his bulletin board.

Allen waives at victory
Dec. 12, 1950

New York - Phog Allen forever tried to change the rules. Sometimes his efforts through the National Association of Basketball Coaches were successful. Mostly, they weren't.

If Phog had his way, there would have been a 12-foot basket and a jump ball after each field goal.

And this rule would have continued after 1952: After a foul teams would have been given an option to shoot the free throws or take the ball out of bounds. Kansas beat the Redmen in Madison Square Garden because Allen waived free throws.

The Jayhawks had passed on their free throws most of the night. They waived 12 opportunities in the first half. Once KU had a double-digit lead, Allen decided to shoot the free ones. St. John's got back in it and again free throws were waived.

St. John's took a 51-50 lead with 50 seconds remaining. At :39, Allen waived a foul. KU took the ball out of bounds under its basket and Bill Hougland's shot bounded around the rim. Lovellette got the tip for the winning points.

For the game, KU waived 26 free throw attempts.

"Teams profit by fouling you," Allen said. "I don't want them to have the ball. I want to show that the foul is too cheap."

It also has something to do with Allen's love of ball-control offense. Whatever the reason, Kansas scored a dramatic non-conference victory and Allen believed he made his point.

Kansas 90, Kansas State 88, OT

KU works overtime for holidays
Dec. 28, 1951

Kansas City - Championship teams find ways to win, and the semifinals of the 1951 Big Seven Holiday Tournament provided the Jayhawks a chance to win ugly.

Kansas lost all of a 19-point, first-half lead and had to hold off the charging Wildcats in overtime.

The Jayhawks led 28-19 after one quarter, 42-23 with four minutes left in the half and 49-35 at halftime. K-State started to peck away in the third quarter, but Kansas seemed safe with a nine-point lead heading into the final period.

But behind Jim Iverson and Jack Carby the Wildcats roared back. Less than four minutes into the quarter, K-State took a 67-66 lead. Now it was anybody's game.

Clyde Lovellette scored from inside with 14 seconds remaining for an 80-78 lead. Five seconds later, Bill Lienhard committed a foul, but the Wildcats elected to take the ball out of bounds rather than shoot the free throws.

The in-bounds pass was batted around the basket before K-State's John Gibson tipped it in just before the final buzzer.

In overtime, the teams traded hoops until Lovellette dropped in a hook for a 90-88 lead with 1:52 remaining. That ended the scoring. Kansas got the ball back after a K-State miss and ran off all but the final four seconds.

Lovellette came up big, scoring 22 of his 27 points after he had picked up his fourth foul.

The victory made KU 9-0 and was its biggest of the season. The Jayhawks proved they could win under adverse conditions.

Kansas 75, Missouri 65

Lovellette "kicks" Tigers
Dec. 29, 1951

Kansas City - Phog Allen didn't have many close friends in the coaching business who hadn't either played or coached for him. But Allen made a new buddy in the championship game of the 1951 Big Eight Holiday Tournament under the most unusual of circumstances.

Missouri coach Sparky Stalcup wasn't a big Allen fan. They nearly came to blows during a 1947 game in Lawrence, Stalcup's first visit to Kansas as the Tigers' head coach. But Stalcup's actions during the end of the Jayhawks' victory became the basis for a long friendship.

With three minutes remaining, KU center Clyde Lovellette drove his right foot into the gut of a sprawled out Tiger Win Wilfong. Nearly 10,000 in Municipal Auditorium, including many Kansas fans, booed Lovellette. He was ejected and later admitted his mistake.

"He had climbed on my back," Lovellette said. "I got a rebound and put it back in, then I shook him off like a dog shakes water off his back. He fell to the ground, and, I don't know why, but I planted my size 14 right in his stomach."

The booing lasted the rest of the game and during the awards ceremony. When Lovellette went to the Missouri bench to shake Wilfong's hand, Stalcup intercepted him and shook his hand. Stalcup then came to the microphone and said "The University of Missouri enjoys this rivalry with the University of Kansas. Doc Allen is a great coach."

Missouri players then went to the Kansas bench to shake hands. Wilfong and Lovellette hugged. Allen was stunned. His respect and admiration for Stalcup grew that night.

TCU pushes KU to brink
March 21, 1952

Kansas City - Kansas' quest for the 1952 NCAA championship nearly didn't advance beyond the first round.

The Jayhawks opened a huge fourth quarter lead and withstood a furious rally by Texas Christian to post the narrow triumph.

Kansas led 62-44 two minutes into the fourth quarter. TCU scored 10 straight to get the Jayhawks' attention. Clyde Lovellette knocked in six straight, the last with 2:49 remaining and Kansas appeared home free.

Not so fast. The Horned Frogs went on another 10-0 spree but time ran out. TCU fans rang their cowbells and were joined in the cheering by fans of the other regional semifinalists, St. Louis and New Mexico State.

The game was poorly played on both sides. Lovellette scored 31 to tie an NCAA Tournament record and set the mark for a Western playoff. Jayhawk guard Bob Kenney added 17, but nobody else stood out for the Jayhawks.

TCU's George McLeod, who led the Southwest Conference in scoring, fouled out in the first half.

The teams shot horribly, with Kansas hitting 28-of-73 (38.4 percent) and the Horned Frogs 26-of-74 (35.1 percent). But the Jayhawks had Lovellette, the best player in the college game in 1952, and that was enough to get the postseason quest off to a winning start.

Clyde Lovellette (16) tangles with Texas Christian in the 1952 NCAA Tournament.

Big Clyde's best launches KU to finals
March 22, 1952

Kansas City - This is what college basketball in Kansas City was like in 1952:

Moments after the Jayhawks victory over St. Louis that propelled Kansas into the national semifinals, a conga line snaked north on Wyandotte Street and Baltimore Avenue. It was 22 degrees.

Downtown hotel lobbies were jammed, more than 1,000 crowded the lobby of the Muehlebach alone. The Kansas City Club, a dinner club, drew its biggest crowd in five years.

All because Kansas whipped the Billikens. This was a victory worth celebrating.

St. Louis was ranked fifth, the Jayhawks eighth. But Municipal Auditorium was packed with Kansas fans wearing white sweaters.

The Billikens came in with a strategy, cut off the outside and hope Clyde Lovellette was off his game. Big mistake.

Lovellette scored an NCAA Tournament record 44 points. He made 16 of 28 from the floor. No KU player had more than four field goals. The night before against Texas Christian, Lovellette had tied the single-game scoring record of 31 points, set by North Carolina's George Glamack in 1941.

The Jayhawks needed Big Clyde. St. Louis came out on fire and led 14-8 after one quarter. The game was tied several times in the second quarter, including 27-27 at halftime. Lovellette had 19 at the break.

Thirty seconds into the third quarter, Lovellette scored from inside for a 29-28 lead. Kansas didn't trail again. But the Jayhawks didn't pull away until early in the fourth quarter.

Lovellette raised his scoring average to 27 points. It had been steadily rising late in the season and while no national college player of the year was selected until 1955, Big Clyde was clearly proving there was no more valuable player in the game.

Clyde Lovellette with "Phog" Allen.

Action from 1952 championship game against St. John's.

Lovellette leads return to final
March 25, 1952

Seattle - The 1952 NCAA Tournament marked the first year of four regions and a Final Four setting. For the first 13 championships, an Eastern and Western champion met at one site, usually Kansas City or New York.

The 1952 semifinals pitted St. John's against Illinois and Kansas against the event's surprise team, Santa Clara. The Broncos were seen as no better than the third best team in the West, behind Wyoming and UCLA. But Santa Clara whipped them both with a team that started three freshmen.

This one was over early. The Jayhawks led 18-10 after one quarter, 38-25 at halftime and 59-39 at the end of three quarters. Clyde Lovellette scored 33, his fifth straight game over 30.

The real excitement happened before the game. First, the plane ride to the West Coast. The Jayhawks' flight was in a holding pattern because of bad weather and was running low on fuel. Lovellette took some flowers from a vase on the wall, handed them to Phog Allen and according to lore said "Relax, Doc. If we crash, you've got on a good suit and they can take you right to the funeral home."

Lovellette was involved in another scare. The night before the game, he received permission to have dinner with a fraternity friend on a Navy cutter. A thick fog rolled in and the boat couldn't make it back.

"It got later and later and later," Lovellette said. "The fog lifted early in the morning and we finally got back. It was morning when I got some sleep."

Allen, who had punished players for missing curfews, excused Lovellette, and as usual, he dominated the game. No Bronco could match up with him. Lovellette used his hook shot repeatedly and was out of the game with eight minutes remaining.

Kansas had reached the title game for the second time. In fewer than 24 hours, the Jayhawks would play for the national championship.

The 1952 national championship team: Front row (left to right): Dean Kelley, Ken Buller, John Thompson, Don Anderson, Dean Smith, Jack Rodgers, Allen Kelley. Second row (left to right): Wayne Louderback (student manager), LaVennes Squires, Everett Dye, Bob Godwin, Larry Davenport, Phog Allen, Bob Kenney, Wes Whitney, Wes Johnson, Dean Wells. Back row (left to right): Dick Harp (asst. coach), John Keller, Bill Heitholt, Bill Hougland, B.H. Born, Clyde Lovellette, Bill Lienhard, Wally Beck, Charlie Hoag, Dean Nesmith (trainer).

Look of a champion
Mar. 26, 1952

Seattle - St. John's stood between Kansas and its first NCAA championship, and the Jayhawks had to feel confident. A season earlier, KU had knocked off the Redmen in New York. This was a better St. John's team but a much better Jayhawks team.

St. John's had earned its title shot. The Redmen defeated Kentucky in a regional semifinal by seven. Earlier in the year, the Wildcats had defeated St. John's by 41 in Lexington, in a game that featured the first black player on the floor at Kentucky, the Redmen's Solly Walker. Revenge was sweet. Kentucky had won 23 straight and was ranked No. 1 entering that game.

The Redmen knocked off second-ranked Illinois in the semifinals. Kansas, ranked eighth, avoided playing either No. 1 or No. 2 for the title. St. John's was ranked 10th.

The championship game was a rout from the start. The Jayhawks opened a 7-1 lead, led 18-13 after one quarter and 41-27 at halftime. St. John's never got closer than 11 in the second half.

Mostly, it was a foul-fest. Sixty fouls were called, 35 by the Redmen. Kansas went to the line 35 times and St. John's 27.

Clyde Lovellette finished with 33 points and 17 rebounds and is the only player in Division I history to lead the nation in scoring (28.4) and play for a championship team in the same year.

Lovellette finished with 13 NCAA Tournament scoring records, including points (141) and rebounds (69) in a series. After an 11-year absence, the all-tournament team was reinstated and Lovellette was an easy choice for most valuable player.

Never known for his defense, Lovellette came up big against the Redmen. Counterpart Bob Zawoluk finished with 20, but he had only six at halftime as Kansas set the tone.

At 66 and already basketball's winningest coach, Phog Allen at last had his championship. But there was more work to be done. This was an Olympic year and Allen had promised his seniors a chance for a gold medal.

Clyde Lovellette on his initial reaction to Kansas

66 Everything I did was geared toward going to Indiana. Everybody knew who Branch McCracken was. I had never heard of Phog Allen. 99

1952 NCAA championship box

Kansas

	FG-A	FT-A	R	A	F	TP
Bob Kenney	4-11	4-6	4	2	2	12
John Keller	1-1	0-0	4	1	2	2
C. Lovellette	12-25	9-11	17	2	4	33
Bill Lienhard	5-8	2-2	4	1	4	12
Dean Kelley	2-5	3-6	2	1	5	7
Charlie Hoag	2-6	5-7	4	1	5	9
Bill Hougland	2-5	1-3	6	0	2	5
L. Davenport	0-0	0-0	0	0	1	0
Bill Heitholt	0-0	0-0	0	0	0	0
B.H. Born	0-0	0-0	0	0	0	0
Allen Kelley	0-2	0-0	1	0	0	0
Totals	28-63	24-35	42	8	25	80

St. John's

	FG-A	FT-A	R	A	F	TP
Jack Machon	6-12	1-4	22	2	4	13
Jim Davis	1-4	2-3	2	0	4	4
Bob Zawoluk	7-12	6-11	9	1	5	20
Dick Duckett	2-5	2-2	2	0	4	6
R. MacGilvray	3-8	2-5	10	5	3	8
Jim Walsh	3-6	0-0	4	0	3	6
Solly Walker	0-2	0-0	2	3	4	0
J. McMorrow	1-3	0-0	0	0	3	2
Phil Sagona	2-2	0-0	0	0	5	4
F.Giancontieri	0-0	0-2	1	0	0	0
Carl Peterson	0-1	0-0	0	0	0	0
Totals	25-55	13-27	32	11	35	63

KANSAS	18	23	19	20	80
ST. JOHN'S	13	14	14	22	63

Officials: Lightner, Shaw.
Attendance: 10,700

The 1952 Jayhawks arrive home
with the NCAA championship trophy.

A Century of Jayhawk Triumphs

Play by play of the 1952 NCAA championship game

First quarter		KU	St. John's
Lovellette	FT	1-0	
Keller	follow	3-0	
Davis	FT		3-1
Lienhard	jumper	5-1	
Kenney	jumper	7-1	
Zawoluk	2 FTs		7-3
Lovellette	inside	9-3	
MacGilvray	inside	9-5	
Duckett	drive		9-7
Lovellette	FT	10-7	
Zawoluk	inside		10-9
Kenney	outside	12-9	
Zawoluk	inside		12-11
Kelley	tip	14-11	
Lovellette	tip	16-11	
Lovellette	inside	18-11	
McMahon	jumper		18-13

Second quarter		KU	St. John's
Hougland	jumper	20-13	
Walsh	jumper		20-15
Lovellette	tip	22-13	
MacGilvray	inside	22-17	
Hougland	jumper	24-17	
Walsh	jumper		24-19
McMahon	layup		24-21
Lovellette	inside	26-21	
Lovellette	FT	27-21	
Lienhard	jumper	29-21	
Lienhard	jumper	31-21	

		KU	St. John's
Walsh	jumper		31-23
Lovellette	inside	33-23	
Kenney	tip	35-23	
Lovellette	FT	36-23	
Duckett	2 Fts		36-25
Lienhard	jumper	38-25	
Lienhard	FT	39-25	
MacGilvray	inside	39-27	
Hoag	layup	41-27	

Third quarter		KU	St. John's
Zawoluk	FT		41-28
Lovellette	2 Fts	43-28	
Kenney	FT	44-28	
Lovellette	FT	45-28	
MacGilvray	FT		45-29
Lienhard	jumper	47-29	
Davis	tip		47-31
Davis	FT		47-32
Lovellette	FT	48-32	
Zawoluk	FT		48-33
McMahon	FT		48-34
Zawoluk	inside		48-36
Zawoluk	FT		48-37
Kenney	FT	49-37	
Lovellette	tip	51-37	
McMahon	jumper		51-39
Lovellette	hook	53-39	
Lovellette	hook	55-39	
Lienhard	FT	56-39	
McMorrow	jumper		56-41

		KU	St. John's
Kenney	FT	57-41	
Hoag	FT	58-41	
Hoagland	FT	59-41	
Hoag	FT	60-41	

Fourth quarter		KU	St. John's
Zawoluk	layup		60-43
Lovellette	hook	62-43	
Zawoluk	layup		62-45
Kenney	jumper	64-45	
Kenney	2 FTs	66-45	
Zawoluk	FT		66-46
Sagona	jumper		66-48
Kenney	FT	67-48	
Zawoluk	inside		67-50
Hoag	FT	68-50	
Zawoluk	inside		68-52
Duckett	jumper		68-54
Hoag	layup	70-54	
MacGilvray	FT		70-55
Lovellette	tip	72-55	
Hoag	FT	73-55	
McMahon	inside		73-57
Lovellette	FT	74-57	
McMahon	jumper		74-59
Kenney	jumper	76-59	
Sagona	jumper		76-61
Lovellette	tip	78-61	
McMahon	inside		78-63
Kenney	FT	79-63	
Hoag	FT	80-63	

1952 Olympic team.

Front Row (L to R): Dean Kelley, Charlie Hoag, John Keller, Bob Kenney, Bill Houghland, Bill Lienhard, Clyde Lovellette.

Back Row (L to R): Dr. F. C. (Phog) Allen, Bob Kurland, Marcus Freiberger, Frank McCabe, Ron Bontemps, Wayne Glasgow, Dan Pippin, Howie Williams, Warren Womble.

On to Helsinki
March 31, 1952

New York - The Jayhawks had won the national tournament. Now they were out to conquer the world.

The Olympic playoffs started only four days after Kansas had won the NCAA Tournament.

The Jayhawks dusted off NAIA champion Southwest Missouri State 92-65 in Kansas City and qualified for a trip to Madison Square Garden, where NIT champion La Salle awaited.

This was the big game in Olympic qualifying. The winner would provide half of the team that would represent the United States in Helsinki. There would be one more game for the winner, to determine the head coach. But a loss to La Salle would mean no Olympics for Kansas.

Phog Allen wasn't about to take any chances. The team was prepared to depart Kansas City when Allen got word that no official from the Midwest had been contracted for the playoff. The Jayhawks weren't coming without one. Olympic officials agreed and an area referee accompanied the team on the plane.

La Salle was led by freshman whiz Tom Gola, who in the next three seasons would become national player of the year and lead the Explorers to the 1954 NCAA title.

Gola nearly added an Olympic berth to his resume. Before 11,179 at the Garden, La Salle dominated the first half.

They raced to leads of 24-14 and 40-29. The Jayhawks trailed by five at halftime. The contest was played in quarters, and the Explorers led 54-49 heading into the fourth.

Then Clyde Lovellette took over. He scored 12 straight, personally turning a 57-55 deficit with seven minutes to play into a 67-61 lead with two minutes remaining.

The game was over. In his last game against a college opponent, Lovellette had scored 40 and grabbed 14 rebounds. He had scored more in a game but Lovellette had never come up bigger. "Lovellette is the greatest big man I've ever seen in the collegiate game," said New York Knicks coach Joe Lapchick, who also coached St. John's for 20 years. "He's even stronger than George Mikan."

Lovellette left New York on a sour note. Kansas never led in the Olympic playoff title game against the Peoria Caterpillar Diesels. But with a chance to take the lead in the final seconds, Lovellette went the length of the floor for a layup. But he went up too soon and the ball banged off the back iron. Peoria then got a quick hoop for a two-point victory.

The outcome meant Allen would be the assistant and not Olympic head coach. But that was fine with Allen. The Jayhawks were going to Helsinki.

Jayhawks in the Olympics

Thanks to Phog Allen, basketball became an Olympic sport in 1936. He had kept tabs of international basketball's growth through Naismith, who had corresponded and traveled around the world watching nations interpret his game.

The 1936 team was selected through an eight team playoff in New York that included five from college ranks, two from the AAU and one from the YMCA. The playoff finalists would supply 13 of the 14-man roster. College teams would qualify by winning district playoffs.

Kansas, with three all-Big Six players, looked like a good bet to reach New York. The Jayhawks finished the regular season 18-0, then defeated Washburn and Oklahoma A&M in Olympic district playoffs. All Kansas had to do was defeat unheralded Utah State twice to reach New York.

But after defeating the Aggies in overtime in the opener, the Jayhawks dropped two straight. While the first Olympic team would be well represented by Kansans - six players and an assistant coach from the McPherson Globe Oilers - none were from Lawrence.

Beginning with the next Games, in 1948, a Jayhawk represented the United States in the next four Olympics and five of the next six. Kansas' 12 basketball Olympians are the most from any school.

The Jayhawks supplied half the 1952 team when Kansas won the NCAA title and defeated NIT champion La Salle for the college Olympic playoff. Allen went to Helsinki as an assistant coach.

Bill Hougland, a starter for the NCAA champions, also was selected to the 1956 Olympic team.

Danny Manning, who made the 1988 team, is the latest KU Olympian. He and Darnell Valentine, selected for the

1980 team that boycotted the Games, are the only Jayhawks not to win gold medals.

Besides Clyde Lovellette's performance in 1952, the most valuable Kansas player in an Olympics was Jo Jo White in 1968. It was an American team more noteable for who wasn't there - namely UCLA's Lew Alcindor and LSU's Pete Maravich - than who was.

There also was a feeling the United States may lose its first game in the Olympics. Yugoslavia and especially the Soviet Union were catching up with the Americans. But a USA-USSR showdown never occurred. Yugoslavia upset the Russians for the right to meet Coach Hank Iba's Americans for the gold medal.

The United States led 32-29 at halftime, but White and Spencer Haywood scored eight points each in a 17-0 run to open the second half and put away the game. White averaged 11.7 points in nine games, second to Haywood's 16.1 average. Only Lovellette, who average 14.1 points in 1952, posted a higher average among Jayhawks in the Olympics.

Jayhawks in the Olympics

Gordon Carpenter	1948
Charles Hoag	1952
Bill Hougland	......1952, 1956
John Keller	1952
Allen Kelley	1960
Dean Kelley	1952
Robert Kenney	1952
Bill Linehard	1952
Clyde Lovellette	1952
Danny Manning	1988
Darnell Valentine	1980
Jo Jo White	1968

Kansas-led Olympians grab gold
July 31, 1952

Helsinki - Time was at hand for Phog Allen to deliver on a promise.

Four years earlier, when he recruited players like Clyde Lovellette, Bill Hougland and Bob Kenney, Allen said that during their senior season they would win the NCAA championship and the Olympic gold medal.

With seven members of the NCAA champion Jayhawks representing their country, the United States cruised to the final against the Soviet Union, participating in its first Olympics. The U.S. already had routed Russia, 86-58 in the fourth of eight games. The Soviets knew they couldn't play uptempo again and win.

Russia had taped its earlier loss and charted every detail of the game. The only chance to stay close was to slow the pace to a crawl. The United States led only 17-15 at half-time and trailed 21-20 three minutes into the second half.

But there were plenty of Americans who knew something about these tactics. Kansas under Allen was more methodical than uptempo, and Bob Kurland, who played for ball control artist Hank Iba at Oklahoma A&M, wasn't seeing a stall for the first time.

Kenney's two free throws restored the lead for the United States and the Americans weren't fronted again. Baskets by Lovellette, Kenney and Kurland put the game away. Hoagland had kept the Americans alive in the first half with three straight baskets, including the final one to give the U.S. its halftime lead

The United States got in a final dig. With a double-digit lead and the ball in the final minutes, the U.S. went into a stall. Russian players sat down on the floor until the Americans made a move to the basket.

The United States went 13 for 54 from the field (24 percent) while the Soviets finished eight of 29 (27.4 percent).

In eight Olympic games, the Jayhawks usually played together. Lovellette led the team in scoring at 14.1 points and Kenney was second at 10.9. Lovellette's nine led the United States in the title game, but it hadn't been an easy win. After the third game, Olympic coach Warren Womble benched Lovellette and played Kurland with the KU players.

"Lovellette isn't playing well," Womble said. "How much Lovellette plays will depend on how much he works."

Lovellette got the message. He sat out the third game against Uruguay. If the benching was a motivational ploy, it worked. Big Clyde scored 14 against the Soviets and knocked out Russia's best player, Otar Korkiia, while scrambling for a loose ball.

With Kansas players going most of the way in the fifth game, Lovellette scored 25 as the United States beat Chile 103-55.

By now, Lovellette was the team's most important player. He led the U.S. with 11 points in its closest game of the tournament, 57-53 over Brazil, a game in which the Americans trailed 30-26 early in the second half.

Against Argentina, for a right to play for the gold medal, the United States won 85-76 and got 25 from Big Clyde.

The Jayhawks didn't figure prominently early in the Games, but they got most of the playing time toward the end. The 1952 Olympics were the last in which one college provided half the team. Fittingly, that team was Kansas.

1952 Olympic results and leading scorers

United States 66, Hungary 48	Dan Pippin (Missouri) 15
United States 72, Czechoslovakia 47	Bob Kurland (Oklahoma A&M) 12
United States 57, Uruguay 44	Kurland 21
United States 86, Soviet Union 58	Bob Kenney, Clyde Lovellette 14
United States 103, Chile 55	Lovellette 25
United States 57, Brazil 55	Lovellette 11
United States 85, Argentina 76	Lovellette 25
United States 36, Soviet Union 25	Lovellette 9

Roster

Ron Bontemps	G	Peoria Caterpillars (Illinois, Beloit)
Marcus Freiberger	C	Peoria Caterpillars (Oklahoma)
Wayne Glasgow	F	Phillips 66ers
Charlie Hoag	F	Kansas
Bill Hougland	G	Kansas
John Keller	F	Kansas
Dean Kelley	G	Kansas
Bob Kenney	F	Kansas
Bob Kurland	C	Phillips 66ers (Oklahoma A&M)
Bill Lienhard	F	Kansas
Clyde Lovellette	C	Kansas
Frank McCabe	F	Peoria Caterpillars (Marquette}
Dan Pippin	G	Peoria Caterpillars (Missouri}
Howie Williams	G	Peoria Caterpillars (Purdue}

Other Jayhawks in the Olympics

1956 Melbourne
Bill Hougland

1960 Rome
Allen Kelley

1968 Mexico City
Jo Jo White

Dean Nesmith, trainer

1980 Moscow (boycotted by U.S.)
Darnell Valentine

1988 Seoul
Danny Manning

Bill Hougland

Allen Kelley started for the 1953 NCAA finaists and was a member of the 1960 Olympic team.

Jo Jo White drives in the 1968 Olympics.

K-State streak ends
Feb. 17, 1953

Manhattan - Kansas State ruled the Big Seven in 1951. Kansas in 1952. The Wildcats were on their way to regaining the upper hand in 1953. They had defeated the Jayhawks in the Holiday Tournament and although K-State had lost in Lawrence, it only needed to protect its home floor against KU for the upper hand in the league race.

The Jayhawks stood 6-2 and the Wildcats 4-2 heading into their meeting at Ahearn, where K-State had won 27 straight, including 15 in the conference.

The game was tight throughout with 11 ties and 16 lead changes. Neither side led by more than six.

K-State led 40-39 at halftime but Dean Kelley scored eight straight points early in the third quarter to give Kansas a 53-47 lead. He fouled out

late in the third quarter, and the Jayhawks went back to their star, Born, who finished with 27.

Kansas led most of the second half and looked like winners when B.H. Born's layup made it 79-75 with 1:50 remaining. But Kansas State closed to one when Gary Bergen scored on a tip-in and free throw.

The Wildcats got the ball back and played for a final shot. With 10 seconds remaining substitute guard Bob Smith was fouled. He missed them both. K-State missed 26 free throws for the game.

The Jayhawks' Dean Smith made one of two from the line with eight seconds remaining - his only point of the game - to close the scoring.

K-State's Dick Knostman also had 27, but it wasn't enough to keep the pendulum of power in the Big Seven from swinging back to the Jayhawks.

B. H. Born.

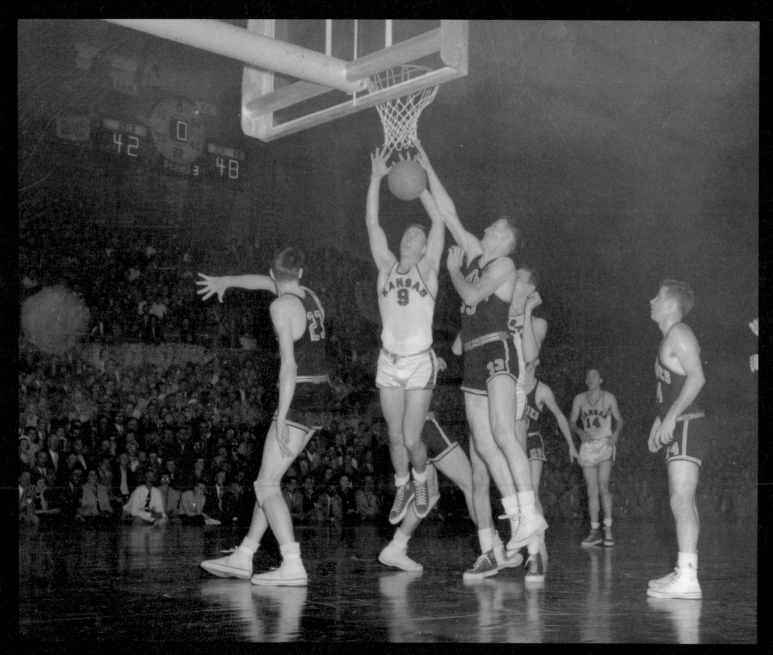

Gil Reich goes strong to the basket in the 1953 regional contest against Oklahoma A&M.

Heart pumps KU into finals
March 14, 1953

Manhattan - By the time Kansas and Oklahoma A&M met for the 1953 regional championship, the programs had clearly established prominence in college basketball. The Aggies had been to four national finals since 1946. Kansas had won the 1952 title. Games between the Jayhawks and Aggies pitted legendary coaches Phog Allen and Hank Iba.

The 1953 regional was well played and uncharacteristically high scoring for Allen and Iba coached teams. But that had been the trend in their regular-season meetings. KU won in Lawrence 65-53 and the Cowboys in Stillwater 79-58, by far the most points scored by Oklahoma A&M in the previous 32 meetings.

The 21-point game, played three weeks before the playoff, was fresh in the Jayhawks' minds. Phog Allen made sure of that. It had been the most lopsided loss of the season.

Kansas was ranked sixth and the Cowboys seventh. KU jumped to a 30-28 halftime lead and started to pull away in the second half before getting into foul trouble. Center B.H. Born scored 18 before fouling out.

The Jayhawks, with nobody taller than 6-2 Gil Reich on the floor in the final minutes, held on for the victory. Reich was guarding 6-11 Bob Mattick, who finished with 22 points and eight rebounds.

But Kansas countered with Dean Kelley. He scored 10 of his 16 in the third quarter.

"He won it," Phog Allen said. "He broke it open. He's always been a great competitor."

Mostly, Allen was thrilled with the team. Kansas had lost four starters off the national championship team but now was headed for the finals in Kansas City.

"I don't believe it, I just don't believe it," Allen said. "I've never had as much joy or pride in a club as this one. It was so unexpected. We haven't got the size, we haven't got the power, but we've got the heart."

B.H. Born defends the basket in the 1953 NCAA semifinal against Washington.

Early blitz zips Washington
March 17, 1953

Kansas City - Clyde Lovellette's NCAA Tournament record of 44 points against St. Louis in 1952 didn't last long. Washington's Bob Houbregs scored 45 in a 1953 West Regional semifinal victory over Seattle.

The Huskies blew into the national semifinal as the nation's fourth-ranked team and were favored by three over Kansas. But coach Phog Allen gave one of the most emotional pregame speeches of his career and the Jayhawks jumped to an 8-0 lead.

Washington was stunned. Coach Tippy Dye's Huskies had come in confident with a terrific 29-2 record. They had been advertised as one of the best teams produced in the West. Houbregs hook shot was unstoppable.

But it's tough to score when you can't shoot, and Kansas had eight points before Washington had crossed midcourt. It took six possessions before the Huskies got a field-goal attempt. For the game, Kansas unofficially came up with a remarkable 21 steals.

Finally, the Huskies calmed down. They caught Kansas at 16-16 and took the only lead of the game at 18-17 on a Houbregs hook shot. Soon, the Jayhawks led 39-29 and the margin grew to 11 at halftime.

Houbregs, one of the nation's top players, fouled out early in the third quarter. It was only the third disqualification in the senior's career. He finished with 18 but was no match for his counterpart, B.H. Born.

Born started only as a senior for the Jayhawks but admirably filled Clyde Lovellette's role. Kansas replaced four starters from the 1952 title team but Born's play - he led the Big Seven in scoring at 22.5 points - made the transition smoother.

Born scored 25 against Washington. Although the Jayhawks lost in the final to Indiana, Born was named MVP of the Final Four.

The victory was the last in the NCAA Tournament for Allen. Kansas shared the league title in 1954 but didn't make the field. Allen's career concluded with a 10-3 NCAA Tournament record with one championship and two trips to the championship game.

The 1953 Jayhawks prepare to board the bus for the short trip to Kansas City and the NCAA Tournament.

It may be the most famous address in college basketball: Allen Field House on Naismith Drive.

On the outside, Allen Field House looks like and old airport hanger. The inside looks and feels like basketball. It's not an arena or coliseum but a simple place, really, with no wasted space. The 16,300 seats are crammed into a building that measures 344 feet by 254 feet.

Coach Roy Williams, who served as a North Carolina assistant in stuffy old Carmichael Auditorium and the spacious Dean Smith Center, calls Allen Field House the best home floor in the game. Even opposing coaches, who seldom win in Lawrence, agree.

"Allen Field House may be the greatest place in college basketball," Oklahoma State coach Eddie Sutton said. "It certainly is one of the most difficult places for a visiting team to win."

Especially in the past 13 years. In that span, there have been seven undefeated home seasons and Kansas owns a 178-14 record. The mark after 42 years is 458-94 (83 percent). From 1984-1988, Kansas won 55 straight at home. The Jayhawks take a 44-game streak into the 1997-98 season.

Even with the largest seating capacity in the Big 12, Allen remains the most intimate building. Fans form a lane and high five players and coaches as they pass over the track from the locker room to the floor. More than 7,000 students stand (never sit) behind the Kansas bench and in the end zone.

Allen Field House came about because Kansas needed a new structure and Kansas State already had one.

Envy had everything to do with a new building. Coach Jack Gardner had turned the Wildcats into winners after World War II and Kansas State opened 11,000-seat Ahearn Field House in 1951. The Jayhawks were still stuffed in 3,000-seat Hoch Auditorium.

Phog Allen wanted a 20,000-seat building that would be large enough to hold a football game in inclement weather. That didn't happen, but he got approval for $2.65 million structure that would seat nearly 17,000.

As completion neared, the name became an issue. There had a been a school policy against naming a building for a living person, although an exception had been made a year earlier. Some wanted to name it for James Naismith, others favored a hyphen job: Naismith-Allen Field House.

But sentiment grew for Allen, and Chancellor Franklin Murphy made the call. Allen Field House was dedicated on March 1, 1955. The Jayhawks defeated Kansas State 77-67 and Allen turned coaching duties over to assistant Dick Harp. More than 100 of Allen's former players returned for the occasion. The announced crowd that night, 17,228, is the largest in KU history.

The scoring records were registered in the first four years. Wilt Chamberlain scored 52 in his Kansas debut in 1956. Two years later, during an NCAA Tournament game, Cincinnati's Oscar Robertson set the building record with 56 against Arkansas.

Largest crowds at Allen Field House

17,228 Kansas State	March 1, 1955	Kansas, 77-67
17,200 Kansas State	March 6, 1974	Kansas, 60-55
17,100 Notre Dame	Jan. 22, 1974	Notre Dame, 76-74

Field House is dedicated to Phog
March 1, 1955

Lawrence - Kansas needed a new building, that was certain. The Jayhawks had long ago outgrown Hoch Auditorium, and there was another factor.

Kansas State.

In 1951, the Wildcats opened 11.200-seat Ahearn Field House. Phog Allen knew the Jayhawks had to keep up.

Allen wanted a 20,000-seat building, large enough to play football if the weather was foul. He didn't get that, but a 17,000-seat structure was approved in 1951. Now, what to call it?

Sentiment was growing for Allen, even though the school was reluctant to name a campus building for a living person. Some favored naming it for James Naismith and other suggested a hyphenated compromise.

In December, 1954, three months before the doors swung open, Chancellor Franklin Murphy determined Allen Field House was a fitting tribute to the long-time coach.

The dedication was spectacular. Every lettermen that could be found was invited and 104 showed up. Allen turned coaching duties to assistant Dick Harp, who understood his job.

"We just couldn't lose that game," Harp said.

The Jayhawks, who entered with a 9-9 record, didn't. Gene Elstun scored 21 and Lew Johnson 20. Kansas didn't trail in the second half but never put away the Wildcats, who closed to 65-62 with 7:42 remaining. Kansas opened a 71-64 lead and stalled away the final three minutes.

"I let Dick run the strategy," Allen said. "I thought it was better for me psychologically to stay out of the picture. I didn't want them doing anything for me but for the spirit of Kansas."

Of course, Kansas did something for Allen, beyond the dedication. The actual ceremony took place at halftime and a program that depicted the history Kansas basketball lasted 35 minutes. Allen was presented keys to a new Cadillac. A building, a car and a victory over the Wildcats. Allen couldn't have wished for a better day.

Phog Allen addresses crowd at halftime of 1955 game with Kansas State that dedicated Allen Field House.

Chapter 5

Dick Harp and Phog Allen.

Dick Harp

8 seasons: 1957-1964
Conference championships: 1957, 1960
Home court: Allen Field House (17,200)

Record: 121-82

Gene Bartow at UCLA felt it. So did Sam Aubrey at Oklahoma State and Joe B. Hall at Kentucky and so will Bill Guthridge, who follows Dean Smith at North Carolina, and those who will follow John Thompson at Georgetown and Bob Knight at Indiana.

Nobody can be prepared for the pressure of following legends like John Wooden, Hank Iba and Adolph Rupp. Expectations are ridiculous. Throw in the added factor of inheriting the game's greatest player, and Dick Harp had double the trouble.

Phog Allen wasn't ready to retire. Harp, Allen's top assistant and former KU standout player, never asked for the job. But when Allen was forced to step down because he had turned 70 before the 1956-57 season, Kansas Chancellor Franklin Murphy appointed Harp as his successor. Allen wanted to stay on for an opportunity to coach his prize recruit, Wilt Chamberlain.

Now Chamberlain would be Harp's player. In their first season together, Chamberlain was everything advertised. He averaged 29.6 points and the Jayhawks had little trouble with the competition. Kansas wasn't perfect, losing at Iowa State and Oklahoma A&M, but the Jayhawks were dominant.

Then came the game that unfairly established reputations for Harp and Chamberlain, the triple-overtime loss to North Carolina in the 1957 NCAA title game.

The Jayhawks had a lead in the second half and decided to stall, allowing the Tar Heels to come back. In the third overtime, a pass to Chamberlain was battled away, sealing North Carolina's triumph.

It didn't seem to matter in Kansas that North Carolina completed a perfect season. Harp was blamed for the defeat. For all his talent, Chamberlain had trouble winning championships, and when his pro teams didn't win, scribes were quick to remind that even in college Chamberlain didn't win the big one.

Such criticism is unfair to both. Harp went on to win another league title in 1960 and coached such stellar players as Bill Bridges and Wayne Hightower. Harp had winning records in five of his eight seasons and won three Big Eight Holiday tournaments.

After a 21-year relationship with Kansas, Harp stepped down at the end of the 1964 season and became head of the Fellowship of Christian Athletes. He lives in Lawrence, attends Kansas games with his season tickets and remains one of the Jayhawks' biggest fans.

Wilt Chamberlain soars for two of his school-record 52 against Northwestern.

It's true: Wilt scores 52
Dec. 3, 1956

Lawrence - Wilt Chamberlain was going to be great, everybody knew that. After all, he had led the freshman team to a victory over the 1956 varsity team the previous year. Now came the first real test, the 1956-57 opener against a Northwestern team that had won its opening game by 39 points.

The Stilt was unbelievable. He went 20 of 29 from the floor and dropped in 12 free throws for a conference-record 52 points. His 31 rebounds set a school record. He broke Clyde Lovellette's record of 44 points with 5:48 remaining and played all but 31 seconds of the contest.

Chamberlain scored the game's first eight points on four baskets and had the Jayhawks' first 11 points before Gene Elstun scored.

The game also marked the debut of coach Dick Harp. Kansas started Chamberlain, Elstun, Maurice King, Lew Johnson and Johnny Parker.

Chamberlain had some troubles with Wildcats' center Joe Ruklick, who managed to get his hook shot over the Stilt

enough times for 22 points. But Northwestern could do nothing with Chamberlain.

Phog Allen, who pulled off the recruiting coup of the century to lure Chamberlain out of Philadelphia, didn't see the game. He gave a speech that night at a high school in Bushton, Kan. During intermission, folks went to the school's lobby to tune in the game on radio. But the audience dutifully returned to hear Phog speak.

"I never will and I do not intend to attend KU games when going will interfere with what I consider to be of more benefit to all concerned," Allen said. "I'll go only when it's convenient."

When word spread of Chamberlain's debut, he was rarely again challenged with one defender. Defenses collapsed, pushed and pulled. Chamberlain went on to finish fourth in the nation in scoring (29.6) and rebounding (18.9). But his scoring total remained a career high and only once, with 36 against Iowa State, did Chamberlain pull down more boards than he did in his debut.

Wilt Chamberlain attempts a free throw during his 1956 varsity debut game against Northwestern.

Wilt Chamberlain in action against Colorado, 1957

Wilt assures NCAA advance
March 15, 1957

Dallas - Wilt Chamberlain scored more points and grabbed more rebounds in a game, but his effort against SMU in his first NCAA Tournament game may have been the most clutch of his career.

Chamberlain scored 36 points and grabbed 22 rebounds, and needed every one of them as the Jayhawks barely reached overtime. The Mustangs had overcome a first-half deficit and made it tight in the second half. There were nine lead changes and three ties after the break. Chamberlain kept Kansas alive by scoring nine straight in a four-minute span.

SMU went ahead 59-57 with 2:17 left in regulation when Ned Duncan buried two free throws. The teams traded possessions before the Jayhawks' Gene Elstun hit a jumper with 32 seconds remaining. The Jayhawks weren't assured of the extra period until Maurice King blocked a shot at the buzzer.

Hounded by the SMU crowd, Chamberlain hit 14 of 26 from the field and eight of 13 from the line. He blocked seven shots.

Kansas caught a break when star Mustangs center Jim Krebs fouled out with five minutes left in regulation.

The Jayhawks dominated the extra period, outscoring SMU 14-6.

Wilt Chamberlain dunks in the annual varsity-freshman game.

Wilt Chamberlain swats a shot verses Oklahoma in 1957.

Tension disrupts regional title
March 16, 1957

Dallas - When Wilt Chamberlain chose to attend Kansas, he asked that no games be scheduled in the South for fear of racial prejudice. The school complied. But it could do nothing about the 1957 Midwest Regional, scheduled for Dallas, or the final opponent, Oklahoma City.

The Jayhawks won easily, earning their first Final Four trip since 1953, but according to one of the game's officials, Al Lightner, the contest was marred by racial taunts and threats and deliberate fouls against Chamberlain and teammate Maurice King.

"The real trouble seemed to be that Chamberlain and King were dark-skinned," said Lightner, who was a sports editor for an Oregon newspaper. "I didn't ask to go down there. They asked me. I didn't travel 2,000 miles to fight the Civil War all over again."

Lightner said that before the game Oklahoma City coach Abe Lemons said if Chamberlain comes down on any of his players they were going to "beat him."

Lemons denied saying anything of the sort and insisted officials were protecting Chamberlain. At one point the game had been stopped because Oklahoma City fans were throwing coins, paper cups, paper airplanes and seat cushions on the floor protesting what they saw as soft officiating.

"It was the toughest seven man zone we played against all year," Lemons said after the game, referring to his team's 25 fouls to the Jayhawks' 10. Kansas shot 42 free throws, Oklahoma City 18.

SMU athletic director Matty Bell pleaded for good sportsmanship over the public address system but the crowd remained stormy throughout.

Oklahoma City was frustrated. It could nothing with Chamberlain, who finished with 30. Ron Loneski had 14 and King 13. Lew Johnson helped Chamberlain on the boards with nine rebounds. Kansas led only 27-24 at halftime but blew it open early in the second half, taking a 15-point lead in the first five minutes.

Kansas was headed for Kansas City and the national semifinals, happy to get out of Texas.

Allen on Wilt Chamberlain's announcement that he would attend Kansas

"I hope he comes out for basketball.**"**

Gene Elstun controls the tap against San Francisco in the NCAA semifinal.

Rout puts Kansas in '57 final
March 22, 1957

Kansas City - San Francisco entered the 1957 Final Four as the two-time defending NCAA champions, but the Dons were something of a surprise to get this far. They upset California to reach the finals and now were matched against formidable Kansas.

A tense bench during the 1957 NCAA semifinal against San Francisco.

The Dons didn't have star center Bill Russell for the first time in three years. But they played a sticky man defense and limited opponents to 55 points per game. And San Francisco entered the national semifinal without an NCAA Tournament loss in 11 games.

It all came crashing down against the Jayhawks, who may have played their best game of the season.

With 10,500 jammed into Municipal Auditorium, Kansas went on a rampage. The game stayed close most of the first half and the Dons trailed only 38-34 at the break.

San Francisco went scoreless over the first four minutes of the second half as Kansas opened a 46-34 lead. The Dons got six straight to slice the margin in half before Kansas put it away with a 16-0 run.

Wilt Chamberlain led the Jayhawks with 32 and Gene Elstun added 16. The Jayhawks made 34 of 57 shots from the field for 59.4 percent while San Francisco was held to 32.4 percent.

The triumph set up the national championship game everybody wanted to see: No. 2 Kansas against top-ranked North Carolina. The Tar Heels had survived in triple overtime in their semifinal against Michigan State.

North Carolina would be tired, Chamberlain was too dominant, the game was in Kansas City. Everything seemed to favor the Jayhawks. But North Carolina won in triple overtime, and it turned out, the victory over San Francisco would be the high water mark in the Kansas careers of Chamberlain and coach Dick Harp.

KU captures playoff
March 9, 1960

Manhattan - As it did so often in the 1960s, the Big Eight championship came down to a Kansas-Kansas State encounter. This was one of the best.

Long before conferences could send more than one team to the NCAA Tournament and before there was a postseason league tournament, only the regular-season winner reached the NCAA.

The Jayhawks and Wildcats tied for the championship with 10-4 records. The teams had split their regular-season encounters, each winning on its home floor. The Big Eight playoff game was set for Ahearn Field House.

Both teams had chances to put it away. The Wildcats led by nine midway through the first half, but the Jayhawks rallied to make it 38-38 at halftime. Kansas took a 13-point lead in the second half, only to have K-State tie it at 72-72 with 2:06 to play. Nobody else scored and the game went into overtime.

KU's Wayne Hightower had been strong throughout the game and finished with 28 points. The extra period heroes were Jerry Gardner and Al Correll. Gardner scored six and Correll four in the overtime. K-State closed the gap to two with seconds left but the Jayhawks ran out the clock.

"We should pass the hat and ask for another three dollars," Dick Harp said. "This crowd got more than it's money's worth."

Kansas remained in Manhattan for the regional, where it defeated Texas and lost to Oscar Robertson and Cincinnati in the final. It turned out to be Harp's last NCAA Tournament appearance.

Wayne Hightower

Roberts' jumper ends marathon
Dec. 29, 1962

Kansas City - Jay Roberts was a football player who didn't figure to see much action in the championship game of the 1962 Big Eight Holiday Tournament against Kansas State. But when 40 minutes didn't settle the outcome, or 45, or 50 or 55, well, it was time for somebody to step up.

Roberts' turnaround one-handed jumper left of the lane swished through the net and ended the longest game in series history. It was Roberts' sixth point, and he really didn't feel comfortable taking the shot. Not with a scorer like Nolen Ellison on the floor.

"When I shot it, I felt real sorry," Roberts said. "I wasn't supposed to do the shooting, and I didn't think I could make it. All I knew was time was running out, and somebody had to throw it up."

There were plenty of heroes for Kansas. Ellison made sure there was a fourth overtime by sinking two free throws with three seconds remaining in the third OT. He finished with 32.

John Matt, who took over when starting center George Ellison fouled out in regulation, scored a key basket in the second overtime and finished with 10.

The victory was especially sweet for Dick Harp. The Jayhawks finished 7-18 the previous year, their worst record since 1929. Kansas now had its first holiday tournament title since 1958, Wilt Chamberlain's final season. KU had won five straight and stood 7-4.

"This one beats all," Harp said. "It's my greatest game as a coach. There's not much I can say about the players. They were all great."

Turns out, the Jayhawks had won on a busted play.

"We messed up the last play," Harp said. "Nolen was supposed to get the shot. But that's not a bad way to mess things up. Jay may not be the best basketball player in the world, but he gets things done."

Harp was swept up in the emotion of the victory. He predicted great things from this team.

"Any group of kids who could do what they did tonight can do anything," Harp said. "We've got to have the same kind of play all season."

But it didn't happen. The Jayhawks finished 12-13, posting successive losing seasons for the first time since the James Naismith teams of 1904 and 1905. For one night, however, Harp and the Jayhawks were euphoric. But it would be the only Kansas victory over Kansas State in an eight-game stretch.

Chapter 6

VCW
INC.

Ted Owens

Ted Owens

19 seasons (1964-1983)   **Record: 348-182**
Conference championships: 1966, 1967, 1971, 1974, 1975, 1978
Homecourt: Allen Field House (15,200)

Ted Owens immediately ingratiated himself to the Kansas fans by winning the Big Eight Holiday Tournament in his first three years. He also won seven of his first eight against Kansas State, which had become the league power.

Owens, an assistant under Harp who was selected over Ralph Miller and Dean Smith, coached more seasons and won more games than any Kansas coach except Phog Allen. He led the Jayhawks during a period of remarkable growth in college basketball and the Big Eight. When Owens started the Final Four was still being played in auditoriums. By the time he left, it had been moved to domes. The Big Eight had been transformed from a league of plodders to sleek athletes.

During Owens' tenure, no team won more than the Jayhawks' six league titles. There were Final Four appearances in 1971 and 1974. The 1971 team, led by Dave Robisch and Bud Stallworth, went 14-0 in the Big Eight and was 27-1 entering the Final Four.

Kansas played UCLA tough in the 1971 national semifinals, recovering from a 13-point halftime deficit, but the Bruins pulled away at the end for an eight-point victory.

Unfortunately for Owens, what many considered to be two of his best teams didn't reach the Final Four.

In 1966, an official waved off what would have been a winning basket by JoJo White against Texas Western in the Midwest Regional title game. White was ruled to have stepped out of bounds. Then, in 1978, Kansas got a lousy draw in the West Regional and lost to UCLA in the opener.

In 1968, the Jayhawks didn't make the NCAA Tournament, but in the first NIT appearance in school history, Kansas reached the title game before losing to Dayton.

Owens was named Big Eight coach of the year four times. Five players were named to an All-America team. He coached 15 academic all-conference players. Owens was fired after the 1983 season. The Jayhawks were coming off seasons of 13-14 and 13-16, but Owens was prepared for a big 1984. Greg Dreiling was coming off a redshirt season and Calvin Thompson was in the fold. But those players would flourish under a new coach, Larry Brown.

Ted Owens on becoming the Jayhawks coach in 1964

66 Elation isn't strong enough to describe my feelings. To find myself as head coach at the finest basketball school in the country is that hard to describe. 99

Holiday win portends Owens' success
Dec. 29, 1964

Kansas City - Kansas turned to 34-year-old assistant coach Ted Owens to take over the program for the 1964-65 season. Players had petitioned for Owens to get the job, and there would be no better opportunity to make a great impression than at the 1964 Big Eight Holiday tournament.

Kansas took a 5-3 record into the event and easily defeated Iowa State in the first round to set up a semifinal date with Kansas State, which had reached the Final Four in the previous year. The Wildcats had won seven of the previous eight meetings with KU.

The Jayhawks led throughout most of the defensive battle, holding a 45-32 edge with 10:45 remaining. Three times, K-State cut the margin to two, but Kansas held on behind the work of junior center Walt Wesley.

The next night, Kansas defeated Colorado 53-51 on Riney Lochmann's tip-in with two seconds remaining for the championship. The Jayhawks and Owens were riding high, and Owens knew the critical game was beating K-State.

"It proved something to me," Owens said. "It proves we're back to the state where we can compete for the championship in our conference. We played the team that is currently the symbol of success in our league and we managed to beat them. This is a great boost for the morale of our kids."

Owens used the holiday tournament as a springboard to a successful season. He captured the event in his first three seasons and four of his first five. In those years, Kansas advanced to the NCAA Tournament or NIT in all but the first.

Walt Wesley

Huskers crumble in showdown
Feb. 26, 1966

Lawrence - In his second season, Joe Cipriano had Nebraska rolling. Behind Grant Simmons and Stu Lantz, the Cornhuskers ended 15 straight years of losing seasons and headed toward their first conference title since 1950.

Nebraska had lost to Kansas in the title game of the Big Eight Holiday Tournament but beat the Jayhawks 83-75 in Lincoln to set up the rubber game in Lawrence. KU was ranked sixth and Nebraska eighth in the most important meeting between the teams in decades.

The Cornhuskers never showed up. Before 17,000, Kansas rolled to a school record point total. The Jayhawks led 58-34 at halftime and coasted to the victory that assured them a tie for the title. Five players scored in double figures, led by Al Lopes with 19. Nebraska made only 21 of 81 from the field.

"Tonight, we were the best basketball team in my two years here," Ted Owens said. "No other night have we been as active and alert for 40 minutes."

Kansas had won its seventh straight and was climbing in the rankings. Owens had started the eligibility of JoJo White at mid-semester because he believed this team could go far and after the victory over Nebraska nobody could dispute him.

Nebraska still could have owned a piece of the championship by winning out and have forced a playoff for the NCAA Tournament berth. But the Cornhuskers lost at Colorado to end the regular season and then fell to Marshall in the first round of the NIT.

Center Walt Wesley doesn't need a ladder to cut the net after the Jayhawks' 1966 victory over Nebraska that clinched the Big Eight championship.

Worst of times for Tark
Dec. 1, 1970

Lawrence - In 1970, Jerry Tarkanian got Long Beach State into the national polls with a 23-3 record and wanted to move the program to a point where it could challenge UCLA. But the 1970-71 season didn't start well for Tark.

The first half proved to be the most futile by an opponent in Allen Field House history. Long Beach made three-of-26 shots and trailed 32-8 at halftime. And the 49ers rallied for that. At one point, they were down 32-4.

"I couldn't believe how tight the kids were," Tarkanian said. "They couldn't even pass the ball much less shoot it or rebound it. Shock is mild word for how I feel right now."

It could have been worse, for everybody. A bomb threat had been called into the building, but officials didn't disrupt the game. Security personnel searched the building and came up with nothing. Much like Long Beach shooters.

The 49ers staged a mild second-half comeback and closed to 56-43, but they ran out of gas as KU pulled away.

The game marked the first for Bud Stallworth as a guard. He had been moved from forward from the previous year and led Kansas with 21 points.

The victory turned out to be one of the Jayhawks' most impressive of their Final Four season. Long Beach finished 16th in the poll, and in the West Regional title game, lost to UCLA 57-55. The 49ers led by 11 with 14 minutes remaining before falling.

Bud Stallworth

Kansas closes Mizzou's Brewer with victory
March 7, 1971

Columbia, Mo. - March 7, 1971 will be remembered for the two heavyweight battles that day. In New York, Joe Frazier won a unanimous decision over Muhammad Ali in the fight of the century.

In Columbia, it was simply another Kansas-Missouri battle. The circumstances surrounding this one gave it a Frazier-Ali electricity.

The Tigers were playing their final game in Brewer Field House, the home floor for 42 years. Missouri was moving into the Hearnes Center the next season. The school had invited letterwinners who had played in Brewer, and 75 were on hand. The building was stuffed, and most of the 6,000 were in their seats two hours before the game.

The Jayhawks were playing for more than nostalgia. Kansas entered the game ranked No. 4 and at 12-0 in the league, was attempting to move one game closer to the first perfect league record since Kansas State in 1958.

It didn't come easily and the game went into overtime. Missouri rode its emotion and Henry Smith, who finished with 24, to the brink of the upset, only to be denied by Dave Robisch.

In the final two minutes of the extra period, Robisch collected an assists, two rebounds and four points to clinch the victory.

Robisch was the difference in the end, but center Roger Brown's contributions early in the second half turned the game. The Tigers led by nine at the break, but Brown scored six points - his only points of the game - and set up two other baskets with assists to give Kansas a 40-38 lead with 16 minutes remaining.

Brown fouled out moments later on a rebound call that disallowed his tip-in.

The game went back and forth from there. Missouri felt good, leading 62-58 with 2:47 left in regulation. Kansas tied it on baskets by Aubrey Nash and Greg Douglas. The Tigers got the final attempt but Greg Flaker missed from the right corner.

Keeping an unblemished conference record was the motivating factor, said Ted Owens.

"It would have been awful easy for our players to say that. Because we had already won the conference, we could just go through the motions," Owens said. "But this is what has made this ballclub. I don't know how many games we've won where the statistics make you feel like you shouldn't have won, but the element of pride has done it time after time."

Dave Robisch

KU holds off inspired Houston in '71 tourney opener
March 18, 1971

Wichita - Kansas entered the 1971 NCAA Tournament on a 19-game winning streak. The lone loss had come at Louisville. Before that game, the Jayhawks blew out Houston by 16 in the Sunflower Classic at Lawrence.

The Cougars remembered the game. There was the added incentive of going home for the Final Four in the Astrodome.

This wasn't the powerhouse Houston teams of the Elvin Hayes-era, but the Cougars were tough behind senior guard Poo Welch, who kept Houston close with his 28 points.

But the Jayhawks countered with Dave Robisch and Bud Stallworth, and they needed both to come up big in the second half.

Stallworth scored 20 of his 25 after the break, helping Kansas overcome a 37-36 halftime deficit. Stallworth had seven points in an 11-0 run that gave KU the lead for good early in the second half.

Houston wouldn't go away. The Cougars closed to 67-65 with four minutes remaining and the margin was a slim 79-76 with 49 seconds to play.

In the days before the three-point shot, Houston could only hope for baskets and stopping Kansas. It happened. The Cougars scored four straight, but the final basket came with three seconds left and Houston couldn't regain possession.

Robisch was huge. He finished with 29 points, 16 rebounds, six blocks and four steals. The Jayhawks had been outshot and outrebounded for the game. Beyond Robisch and Stallworth nobody reached double digits, but they were enough to get the Jayhawks and the 1971 NCAA Tournament quest off to a good start.

Final Four is first since '57
March 20, 1971

Wichita - Drake shouldn't have been in the Midwest Regional title game. The No. 19 Bulldogs had drawn No. 12 Notre Dame in the regional semifinal and everybody had come to see All-America Austin Carr mow down the Missouri Valley champion.

But Drake guard Bobby Jones threw a blanket over Carr, holding him to 26. Not impressed? Carr's outputs in tournament games over the previous two years were 52, 45, 52 and 61. Against Drake, Carr was only 11 of 27 from the floor. The Bulldogs' overtime triumph set up the first meeting with Kansas in 21 years.

Few gave Drake a chance, but it went into the lockerroom at Henry Levitt Arena at halftime with a 38-30 lead. The Bulldogs were throwing their bodies around – three starters fouled out – and the physical play seemed to bother the Jayhawks.

Kansas pushed back in the second half, sometimes too hard. Bud Stallworth fouled out with 14:45 remaining. Pierre Russell was gone with 5:55 left. But that didn't stop the Jayhawks' comeback.

Dave Robisch and Roger Brown took over the offense. Robisch scored 19 of his 27 and Brown 13 of his 15 in the second half. An unsung hero off the bench was Mark Mathews, who came up with a pair of pass deflections in the final two minutes to preserve the Kansas victory.

The Jayhawks won it at the line. Drake closed to one with two minutes to play when Aubrey Nash sank two free throws and Robisch dropped in one.

The victory was the last in Robisch's stellar career. Kansas advanced to the Final Four but lost both games. Robisch finished with 1,754 career points, second at the time only to Clyde Lovellette. Although his senior scoring average of 19.2 points fell off the 26.6 average of his junior year, Robisch enjoyed more team success.

Kansas finished 27-3, perfect in the Big Eight, and had 21 straight victories at one point to tie a school record.

The 1971 Jayhawks finished 27-3 and reached the Final Four. Standing (L-R): trainer Dean Nesmith, head coach Ted Owens, Neal Mask, Randy Canfield, Roger Brown, Dave Robisch, Greg Douglas, assistant coach Gale Catlett, assistant coach Sam Miranda. Seated (L-R): Bob Kivisto, Mark Mathews, Bud Stallworth, Pierre Russell, Jerry House, Aubrey Nash, Mark Williams. Front: manager Kim Blocher.

Stallworth hits half-century mark
Feb. 26, 1972

Lawrence - The 1972 season was drawing to a close and not a moment too soon for the Jayhawks. Ted Owens had clinched his first losing record as Kansas prepared for the home finale against Missouri. The season was a huge disappointment. Better things were expected from a team that finished the previous year 27-3.

But for one game, the losing record was forgotten. Missouri, contending for its first conference championship in three decades, was led by John Brown and Al Eberhard. A victory would allow the Tigers to keep pace with front-runner Kansas State.

Bud Stallworth didn't let it happen. Stallworth shot early and often. When it was over, the Jayhawks had won by 13 and Stallworth had scored 50, a record for points in a Big Eight game.

"I was up for this one," said Stallworth, playing his final home game. "When you're a senior, playing in your last game you've got to give it the best you can."

The Tigers had no answers. They opened the game with 6-0 Mike Griffin on the 6-5 Stallworth. That was a mismatch. Then Missouri coach Norm Stewart switched to 6-4 Mike Jeffries, but that didn't help.

"It's easy to diagnose," Stewart said. "We just didn't play defense."

Stallworth made 19 of 38 shots from the field and 12 of 13 from the line. Owens called it the greatest performance he'd ever seen.

It also was a typical border war. Twice the game had to be halted because of debris on the floor. Stewart collected a technical. Stallworth and Brown got in each other's face. KU fans taunted Missouri players who fouled out.

Stallworth seemed to be releasing a season's worth of frustration in one game. He wound up averaging 25.3 points per game, which ranks as the fifth best season average in KU history. The Jayhawks' second leading scorer in 1972 was Tom Kivisto at 8.9.

Stallworth's mom had come from Alabama to watch her son play for the first time in Lawrence. The 1952 NCAA title team also scheduled its 20th reunion around the game. The season may have been a disappointment, but for one night, everything seemed perfect.

Early hits sink Kentucky
Dec. 3, 1973

Lawrence - Kentucky returned four starters from its 1973 Southeastern Conference championship team and was No. 10 in the preseason poll. The Wildcats had won all five previous meetings with Kansas and most of them weren't close.

It was the perfect chance for Kansas to make a statement. Twelve seconds into the game, Roger Morningstar converted a three-point play and the Jayhawks never trailed. With 10 minutes remaining the Jayhawks had scored 10 straight for a 53-39 lead and weren't threatened again.

Kansas took advantage of the Wildcats' inside weakness. Gone was former all-conference center Jim Andrews. KU big men Danny Knight

with 17 points and nine rebounds and Rick Suttle with 12 points pounded away.

"Their inexperience at the center was the place to hurt them," Ted Owens said.

Kevin Grevey had 24 for the Wildcats but only seven in the first half.

Kansas had taken advantage of the opportunity, beating a big-name opponent and setting the tone for a season that would end with a Final Four trip.

"It was absolutely necessary we play well at this point," Owens said. "We did the things necessary to win against a good opponent."

The 1974 Jayhawks finished 23-7 and reached the Final Four. Front row (L-R): Paul Werner, Reuben Shelton, Dave Traynor, Nino Samuel, Jack Hollis, Bob Emery, Tommy Smith, Tom Kivisto and Dale Greenlee. Back row (L-R): trainer Dean Nesmith, head coach Ted Owens, Roger Morningstar, Donnie Von Moore, Rick Suttle, Danny Knight, Norm Cook, Dale Haverman, assistant coach Duncan Reid, assistant coach Sam Miranda. Front: manager Chuck Purdy.

It's a miracle, KU beats Oral Roberts
March 16, 1974

Tulsa - "Expect a Miracle" is painted on the floor of the Mabee Center at Oral Roberts, and that's just what Kansas got.

The Jayhawks, who trailed by nine with just under five minutes remaining and by seven with 3:19 left, forced overtime then defeated the Titans to advance to the Final Four and a national semifinal date against Marquette.

"Winning in this environment, against a fine team on its court has to be the guttiest thing I've ever seen," Ted Owens said.

Kansas closed fast. Trailing 77-68 with 4:49 left, Roger Morningstar knocked in an 18-footer. Twenty seconds later, Tom Kivisto hit from the top of the circle. After an ORU basket, Dale Greenlee hit a layup. Another ORU hoop, then six straight Kansas points. The Jayhawks had closed to 81-79 with 2:03 left and got the ball when the Titans were called for traveling 30 seconds later.

Norm Cook's jumper pulled Kansas even with a minute left. The Jayhawks had the final possession in regulation but a 35-footer by Greenlee fell short.

Kansas led throughout overtime, but Oral Roberts had the ball down one with 54 seconds remaining. The Titans' Anthony Roberts missed a jumper and the Jayhawks put it away.

Seven played for Kansas and six scored in double figures, led by Danny Knight's 19. The Jayhawks made every big shot down the stretch and finished 40 of 73 (55 percent) from the field.

"I'd like to say there was a great speech made when we were behind," Owens said. "But it was just a matter of these guys knowing what to do, what had to be done and going out and getting it done."

Tar Heel rally falls short
Jan., 3, 1981

Kansas City - North Carolina's visit to Kemper Arena was the first meeting between the Tar Heels and Kansas since the 1957 championship game, in Kansas City's Municipal Auditorium. In 1957, Dean Smith was four years removed from his Jayhawk playing days and throughout his coaching career never liked meeting his alma mater. This game and a return meeting in Charlotte the next year were the only regular-season meetings between Kansas and North Carolina under Smith.

The Jayhawks liked their chances at Kemper. North Carolina was coming off a loss to Minnesota and had trouble shooting over the Gophers' zone. The Jayhawks went with a 3-2 for nearly the entire game.

Al Wood missed 15 of 22 shots, including the potential game-winner from 15 feet. The Tar Heels shot 35 percent from the field.

But Kansas almost gave it away. The Jayhawks led 55-47 with 1:41 remaining, and when Darnell Valentine, who was intensely recruited by North Carolina, hit a free throw with 58 seconds to play the lead was 56-50.

The Tar Heels converted a three-point play. Valentine missed the front end of a bonus with 26 seconds left, and Wood buried two free throws.

North Carolina then fouled the right guy in center Victor Mitchell, a 52-percent shooter from the line. Mitchell missed both with nine seconds left, setting up North Carolina's final chance.

"It wasn't choking up or anything," Mitchell said "I just missed them.'

And fortunately, it didn't cost the Jayhawks a game.

Victor Mitchell challenges North Carolina's Rich Yonaker in a 1981 battle at Kemper Arena.

Darnell Valentine

Starters go the distance for title
Mar. 7, 1981

Kansas City - Four Big Eight postseason tournaments had passed without a Kansas championship. The Jayhawks had reached the title games in 1979 and 1980, but didn't come close to winning.

According to the seeds, the Jayhawks shouldn't have won in 1981. Missouri won the second of four straight championships and was seeded first. Kansas tied for second with K-State and Nebraska and the Jayhawks were seeded fourth.

The Jayhawks knocked out the Tigers in the semifinal and set up a rematch of the 1980 title game with the Wildcats. Ted Owens wanted this one. He made no substitutes, playing tournament MVP Darnell Valentine, Tony Guy, Art Housey, John Crawford and David Magley the entire 40 minutes.

"They were playing so well I saw no reason to change," Owens said. "They were so motivated they didn't become fatigued."

How well were they playing? Kansas shot 55.6 percent from the floor, committed only three turnovers and outrebounded the Wildcats 31-22.

A close game swung Kansas' way with eight minutes remaining. Four different players dropped in a field goal for eight unanswered points.

K-State had played well enough to win. But the Jayhawks headed into NCAA Tournament play with perhaps their best performance of the season.

"I don't know if we've ever had a better performance, at least in my time at Kansas, against as fine a basketball team as this Kansas State team," Owens said.

Who is that Guy?
March 15, 1981

Wichita - Tony Guy never had another game like he did against Arizona State.

Everything fell as Guy scored a career-best 36 and the Jayhawks pulled the upset over the nation's third-ranked team in the second round of the NCAA Tournament.

"This is the greatest moment of my life," said Guy, who connected on 13 of 15 from the floor.

Guy scored Kansas' first points on a 12-foot jumper in transition. Knocking down the first shot keyed Guy's game.

"I felt good shooting it off the break," Guy said. "If I hadn't made a couple of those shots at the beginning, it might have been detrimental."

Guy had 21 in the first half as Kansas led 45-29.

"He saw that we weren't doing much in the begin-ning and he made a response to it," Ted Owens said.

Defensively, the Jayhawks played a swarming zone and threw a blanket around 7-foot center Alton Lister. Kansas could do nothing with Byron Scott, who scored 32.

Scott scored eight straight as Arizona State tried to close the gap in the second half. With 16 minutes to play the KU lead was down to 47-38. But Guy scored four straight, and soon the margin was 17.

Darnell Valentine finished with 18 points, seven assists and three steals. When Guy wasn't scoring, Valentine was.

But Guy, a 6-6 guard who averaged 15.8 points and shot 53.7 percent from the floor in 1981, was the man.

"He was incredible," Valentine said. "I've never seen him play the way he did today. All I had to do was sit back and watch."

Tony Guy

Victory keeps Owens' hopes alive
March 8, 1983

Norman, Okla. - Not until 1986 were all rounds of the Big Eight Tournament played at Kemper Arena. From 1977 until 1985 first-round games were played on campus sites of the higher seeded team, and the Jayhawks found themselves on the road for a difficult assignment in 1983.

There was hope against 19th-ranked Oklahoma. Kansas had defeated the Sooners 55-53 two weeks earlier in Lawrence. But this time the game was at Norman, where Oklahoma had defeated the Jayhawks by 23 in January.

Kansas also had to deal with the distractions. Rumors swirled that Ted Owens was in his final season. Actually, by now athletic director Monte Johnson had all but decided to replace Owens after the season. He, or anybody, didn't expect the season to last after the trip to Oklahoma.

But the Jayhawks, especially freshman Calvin Thompson, couldn't have played better. They jumped on the Sooners early. Kansas couldn't miss, hitting 54 percent from the floor. Thompson scored 30 points on 15 of 20 shooting.

Thompson entered the game with a 9.8 scoring average. "In warmups I wasn't hitting anything, and the coaches were worried about my shot," Thompson said.

KU's Kelly Knight, who had 20 points and 11 rebounds, admitted to cleaning out his locker before the game. "I guess I'll have to bring it all back."

Oklahoma All-America freshman Wayman Tisdale finished with 13 and missed 12 of 18 from the field.

The most satisfied Jayhawk of them all was Owens. He kept his job for four more days.

"I think this has to be, from my standpoint, the most pleasurable game ever," said Owens, who was carried off the floor by the players. "The coaching staff, in my opinion, did an excellent job in the face of frustration."

Larry Brown

Larry Brown

5 seasons (1983-1988)
Conference championship: 1986
National championship: 1988
Homecourt: Allen Field House (15,200)

Record: 135-44

Athletic director Monte Johnson asked Larry Brown to get Kansas back on a winning track. The Big Eight was becoming more competitive: Missouri was in the midst of four straight league championships, Billy Tubbs had arrived at Oklahoma and Johnny Orr at Iowa State. Everybody was getting better.

Naturally, fans wondered how long Brown would stay at Kansas. In his only other college head coaching position, he'd remained at UCLA for two years. He never hung onto an NBA job for more than a couple of years. Five years in Lawrence is the shortest stint for a Kansas coach but until he reached his sixth year with the Indiana Pacers, it was as long as Brown ever held a coaching position.

Brown restored the winning tradition immediately, but his first big victory came in recruiting. He hired, as an assistant, Ed Manning and the Manning family, including son Danny, moved from Greensboro to Lawrence. Two days after the Manning hire, Danny announced he would attend Kansas.

Brown had to coach a season without the complete Manning package. While Danny was helping Lawrence High to a state final, the Jayhawks finished 22-10 and won the Big Eight Tournament.

Then came Danny and four fabulous seasons. KU went 113-34 over the next four years that included a 55-game home-floor winning streak, 1986 league and tournament championship and the 1988 national title.

Four days after beating Oklahoma in Kansas City, Brown agreed to return to UCLA, but 30 minutes before a Lawrence press conference he changed his mind. Brown was staying. And he did - for two more months before he was lured by the San Antonio Spurs.

Brown was the program's most colorful coach since Phog Allen and probably the most superstitious in history. The coaches didn't shave on game days. Paisley ties were forbidden, and coaches could never wear the same tie after a loss.

During the 1988 title run, Brown latched on to a couple of good luck charms. Brown had befriended Ryan Gray, a youngster with an inoperable brain tumor. Gray hung out with the team all year and watched the championship game in the stands with his mother.

Then there was Jimmy Dunlap, the bus driver who got the Jayhawks from their hotel to the Silverdome in Pontiac, Mich. KU had won with him, so Brown had him flown to Kansas City for the Final Four.

No doubt Brown benefitted from excellent timing. The Jayhawks were going to be better in 1984 than in Ted Owens' final season. Greg Dreiling became eligible after transferring from Wichita State. Ron Kellogg and Calvin Thompson had a year under their belts. The nucleus of the 1986 Final Four team was in place.

And it helped to be friends with the Mannings. Brown had coached Ed with the ABA Carolina Cougars in the early 1970s.

But Brown brought an excitement to the program that had been missing for the previous few seasons, and in the end he delivered the ultimate thrill. Five years may have been the prefect tenure.

Larry Brown and Dean Smith

Danny Manning and Larry Brown

Carl Henry

Revenge against Sooners is sweet
March 10, 1984

Kansas City - On Feb. 22, Oklahoma defeated Kansas 92-82 in overtime in Lawrence to clinch the league title. The Sooners taunted the Jayhawks, then cut down the nets in Allen Field House. It was a Billy Tubbs salute to the Big Eight establishment.

The Sooners were the class of the league, winning the championship by four games. They were riding a 13-game winning streak. Kansas had struggled against good teams in Larry Brown's first year, losing big to Kentucky and Houston, which wound up in the Final Four.

But the Jayhawks were primed for this one. Kansas buzzed to a 25-8 lead when Tubbs decided to use freshman scorer Tim McCalister, who had suffered a knee injury in the semifinal victory over Colorado.

Oklahoma crawled back in and looked to be in command with 2:38 remaining when Darryl Kennedy buried a 15-footer for a 78-73 lead. But the Sooners scoring had ended.

Carl Henry, who finished with 30, knocked in two free throws. Kennedy missed the front end of a bonus and Henry hit from the top of the key to make it 78-77. With a minute remaining, OU guard Jan Pannell was looking for Wayman Tisdale when his pass was picked off by reserve center Brian Martin.

Ron Kellogg had missed three straight jumpers. But his 18-footer from the baseline with 41 seconds remaining turned out to be the game-winner.

The Sooners called timeout with 13 seconds left. The idea was to use Tisdale as a decoy and free up guard Shawn Clark for the final shot. But Kennedy found himself with the ball 25 feet from the basket with four seconds left. All rim.

"This means so much to us," Martin said. "We wanted to get them back so bad for what they did to us in Lawrence - the harassing and egging on. If they had won they may have put it in our faces again."

Instead, all Kansas saw were the backs of Oklahoma players while the Jayhawks stayed around to receive trophies.

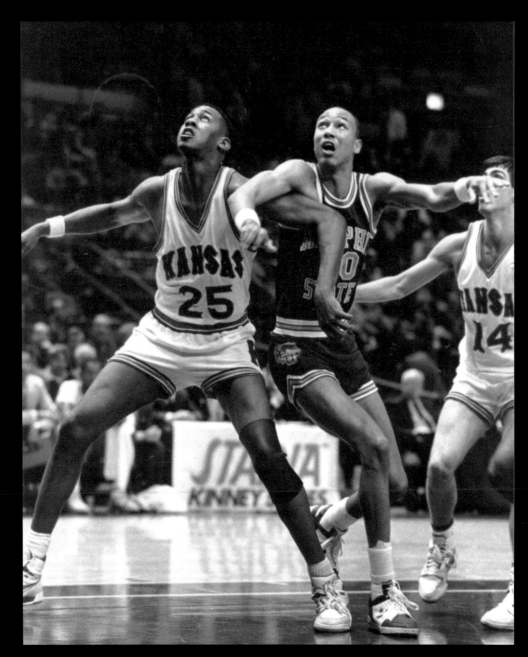

Danny Manning blocks out against Memphis State.

Kellogg tames Tigers
Feb. 9, 1985

Lawrence - Two days before playing third-ranked Memphis State, Kansas had lost by 19 at Michigan. Could Larry Brown beat a major non-conference foe?

The answer came against the Tigers. Brown had the Jayhawks primed and Kansas led by 16 with 10 minutes left. Only when the Jayhawks got cautious did Memphis State get back in it.

The Tigers had closed to four with 1:11 remaining when Ron Kellogg, who should have been winding down the shot clock, missed a jumper. But Memphis State couldn't take advantage and Kellogg was forgiven for his lapse.

Kellogg poured in 34 points on 17-of-27 shooting. Over a span of 7:19 he poured in 16 points. But there were other heroes. Calvin Thompson scored 10 early as KU buzzed to a 16-7 lead, while captain Tad Boyle knocked down both ends of bonus free throws with 33 and 20 seconds remaining to restore four point leads.

Calvin Thompson defends
Memphis State's Vincent Askew.

Boyle had attempted only 13 free throws on the season before the final minute.

Memphis State All-America forward Keith Lee didn't turn it on until the end, scoring 11 of his 22 in the final 10 minutes. The big pain for Kansas was reserve forward Willie Becton, a transfer from St. Louis. Becton entered the game with a 4.1 scoring average and finished with 26.

But Kellogg was the game's top player. He had scored at least 30 for the fourth straight Saturday. He took up the slack for Danny Manning, who had only five in 21 minutes.

"This certainly helps us," Brown said. "Winning a game like this means a lot to our kids and our program. We beat a great team."

One that was headed toward the Final Four.

Senior team buckles down
Nov. 29, 1985

New York - Little did Kansas know when the seasons started, but it wound up playing four games against Final Four teams in 1985-86. The first of these battles came in the Preseason NIT against Louisville.

The Jayhawks had some jitters. Louisville opened the game on a 10-2 run before Kansas caught its breath. Behind Calvin Thompson's shooting, the Jayhawks forged ahead 49-42 at the break.

The Cardinals took a 70-69 lead with five minutes remaining before Kansas made its move. Ron Kellogg scored six points in an 8-2 KU run over the next 2:30 to put it away. Calvin Thompson led the Jayhawks with 25.

The victory set up the title game with Duke, which the Blue Devils won 92-86. But Kansas had proved it could compete with the nation's best. With seniors Kellogg, Thompson and Greg Dreiling along with Danny Manning and Cedric Hunter, the Jayhawks figured this was their best team in years. It certainly ranked with the most disciplined.

In the aftermath of a 26-8 finish in 1985, Larry Brown instituted an off-season curfew. With five starters back, Brown wanted to be sure things wouldn't get lax.

The Jayhawks' performance in the NIT, even with a close loss to Duke, made it obvious Kansas was prepared for the season.

Ron Kellogg

Manning comes home, Kellogg delivers
Dec. 7, 1985

Greensboro, N.C. - For the first time as the Jayhawks coach Larry Brown returned to North Carolina, but the North Carolina State game was more of a homecoming for Danny Manning, who moved from Greensboro to Lawrence while in high school.

Only 6,706 fans showed up in the Greensboro Coliseum but they made their feelings known, booing Brown during the introductions and Manning when he touched the ball.

Ron Kellogg took the heat off both of them. He came up with 23 points, 19 in the second half.

"Kellogg was the ball game," N.C. State coach Jim Valvano said.

Kellogg made nine of 10 field goals in the second half. The matchup was created for television, and that was all right with Kellogg, who through most of his career came up big on national TV. The previous season, the nation saw him score 34 points in games against Memphis State and Oklahoma.

"I feel I can make things happen," Kellogg said. "If I get a shot and nobody's picked me up, I think I can score."

The Jayhawks needed Kellogg's play. The Wolfpack came into the game off losses at Loyola of Chicago and Florida State, but they stayed close throughout the first half behind the play of center Chris Washburn, who had 14 of his 22 before the break.

A two-point Kansas halftime lead grew to 10 with 12 minutes remaining. When N.C. State made a little run, Kellogg answered with a jumper.

"Ronnie was great," Brown said. "He'd be an All-America for any other team in the country, but I hold him back the way we play."

Manning played 35 minutes and finished with eight points and six rebounds, an atypical Manning output. But he would get more opportunities to face his home state team, including a huge one later in the season.

Danny Manning on his decision to attend Kansas

66 (Dean) Smith told me that if I didn't go to North Carolina he wanted me to go to Kansas. 99

Finally, KU tops Kentucky
Dec. 14, 1985

Lawrence - Kansas and Kentucky became regular opponents in the 1970s, much to the delight of the Wildcats.

Starting in 1974, Kentucky ripped off 11 straight victories over KU, including a pair of one-point triumphs in 1978 and 1979. Then there was the overtime decision in 1981 and a three-point margin in 1984.

The 1985 game in Lawrence was the first in the series for new Wildcats coach Eddie Sutton. Kentucky entered with a 5-0 record. But after a close first half, the Jayhawks pulled away.

The Wildcats' leading scorer Kenny Walker was forced out of the game with 16:48 remaining when he took an elbow in the eye from teammate Rob Lock. Walker, who scored 36 in the previous year's game, had 12 this time.

"We probably wouldn't have won by as much had Walker stayed in," Larry Brown said. "But he did play 23 minutes. I think we still would have won if he had played."

True. Kansas got big games from Danny Manning, Calvin Thompson and Ron Kellogg. The Jayhawks shot 61.5 percent from the floor and held Kentucky to 40.4 percent.

To Brown, this one was particularly sweet.

"It means a lot," Brown said. "They have a great coach and great tradition. It gives us something to talk about now when we recruit kids."

Funny that Brown mentioned that. Sutton later said he was no longer interested in continuing the series because the Wildcats didn't recruit in the area. Perhaps it had more to do with his success in Lawrence. Sutton, who also coached at Creighton, Arkansas and Oklahoma State, is 1-8 all time at Allen Field House entering the 1997-98 season.

Rested Dreiling beats Cards
Jan. 25, 1986

Lawrence - In a Preseason NIT meeting between Kansas and Louisville two months earlier, center Greg Dreiling wasn't much of a factor. This time, the Jayhawks wouldn't have won without him.

The Jayhawks nearly didn't get a chance to play with him. Dreiling picked up two fouls in the first 19 seconds of a nationally televised game. He spent the next 19:41 on the bench. A fresh Dreiling had 18 points and five rebounds in the second half.

Dreiling opened the second with three slams. KU had trailed by 13 in the first half was down 36-31 at the break. "We wouldn't have been down like that if Greg had been in there," Ron Kellogg said.

With Dreiling going hard to the basket, Kansas caught the 13th-ranked Cardinals three minutes into the second half. His hook a few minutes later gave the Jayhawks their largest lead at 48-43.

Louisville regained the lead 60-55 but Dreiling led the comeback. Two more dunks contributed to a 6-1 run that tied it. His two free throws with 1:18 remaining all but sealed it.

"He's bigger and stronger than anybody we've got," Louisville coach Denny Crum said. "It's hard to stop a guy that size, especially when he has fresh legs."

The victory pushed seventh-ranked Kansas' homecourt winning streak to 28 games, which tied a school record. It also proved it could beat a quality team motivated by revenge.

"To beat a team like this twice in a year says something about us," Larry Brown said.

KU escapes Cyclones for tourney title
March 9, 1986

Kansas City - Even in its best seasons, Kansas has had trouble against Iowa State. The two most accomplished players produced by the program - Wilt Chamberlain and Danny Manning – went a combined 0-6 at Ames.

But Kansas City and the Big Eight Tournament were the Jayhawks' domain. Kansas was bidding for its third tournament title and Larry Brown's second. For the second straight season, the Cyclones had reached the title game, and they were looking to reverse the two-point loss to Oklahoma the previous year.

Instead, it was more of the same. The Cyclones lost by the same score as the 1985 final, but this time there was controversy. In the final seconds and Kansas holding a two-point lead, two whistles blew. One official, Woody Mayfield, had called traveling on Iowa State's Sam Hill.

Another official, Ron Spitler, had called a foul on Danny Manning, who had grabbed Hill's arm. This all started when a Cedric Hunter pass to Greg Dreiling pass six seconds remaining was knocked away

Calvin Thompson and Ron Kellog hold up the Big Eight championship trophy.

and recovered by the Cyclones' Jeff Hornacek.

Hornacek zipped up floor and spotted Hill in the lane. Then the confusion started. Iowa State claimed Hill should have been at the line with a one-and-one opportunity. But after Mayfield and Spitler conferred, Mayfield said the traveling came first, and there wasn't enough time remaining to run another play. The officials bolted from the floor with Cyclones coach Johnny Orr closely following, cursing them.

"My players hate (Mayfield)," Orr said. "I don't like him. I knew it would come down to a call like this and it would be him."

The ending deflected attention away from a terrific duel between Manning and Jeff Grayer. Manning was named the tournament's MVP with 57 points in three games. But Grayer got the edge in the personal battle in the title game. He finished with 25 to Manning's 23. And Grayer made sure Kansas never pulled too far away by scoring 15 after halftime.

But it wasn't enough to overcome the Jayhawks, and in the Cyclones' minds, the officiating.

Danny Manning tangles with Michigan State in the 1986 regional semifinal.

Like clockwork, Jayhawks beat Michigan State
March 21, 1986

Kansas City - Kansas' victory over

Michigan State in the Midwest Regional semifinal should be remembered for the Jayhawks' stirring comeback in regulation. But it's not.

It will be forever remembered as the clock game, and the Spartans will always believe the malfunctioning ticker in Kemper Arena cost them a shot in the title game.

This is what happened: With 2:21 remaining in regulation, Michigan State's Vernon Carr missed a free throw and made the second to give the Spartans a two-point edge. Kansas brought the ball in but the clock never started. Timer Larry Bates hit the proper switch, but the clock didn't respond.

Several seconds passed when Michigan State coach Jud Heathcote noticed the problem. He charged the scorer's table. By then, the clock had started. Bates had elected not the stop the game to confer with game officials.

With 1:39 remaining, Ron Kellogg picked up his fifth foul. Larry Brown protested to officials that Heathcote should have been charged with a technical foul for leaving the coaching box. As Brown jerked away from an official, his rolled up program hit the whistle of another official, Bob Dibler. Brown picked up a technical. After the free throws, Michigan State held a six-point lead.

Heathcote remained furious and claimed the missing 11 seconds cost him the game. After all, Archie Marshall's game-tying basket on a tip-in came with nine seconds left.

Clearly, Michigan State was unnerved by the incident. The Spartans repeatedly threw away opportunities at the free-throw line in the final two minutes. They missed the front end of two bonus chances, including one with 19 seconds remaining.

Still, Michigan State had a four-point lead with Larry Polec at the free-throw line with 27 seconds left. KU's Danny Manning and Ron Kellogg had fouled out, but the Spartans couldn't close the deal.

In the extra period, Calvin Thompson scored eight of his 26 as the Jayhawks dominated.

The clock had malfunctioned twice a week earlier during the NAIA Tournament and was supposed to have been fixed. A backup clock was used for the Midwest Regional title game. That didn't make Heathcote or the Spartans any happier. They left Kansas City thinking they had been robbed.

Calvin Thompson

Larry Brown cuts the net after KU clinches the 1986 Big Eight championship.

Triumphant Larry Brown after the Jayhawks, 1986 Midwest Regional championship game.

Manning leads Final Four drive
Mar. 23, 1986

Kansas City - For the nation's No. 2 ranked team playing at the friendly confines of Kemper Arena, Kansas still struggled to get out of the Midwest Regional. Michigan State had taken the Jayhawks to overtime. Now North Carolina State was looking like a winner in the title game with nine minutes remaining.

The Wolfpack held a 57-52 lead and it would have been more except Ernie Myers missed a free-throw that would have converted a three-point play.

Danny Manning had seen enough.

"I don't think it was on my shoulders, but I knew if I got the ball I could make things happen," Manning said.

Which is precisely what happened. Manning scored 12 straight points to change the game. In order: a 15-footer,

layup around Chris Washburn, follow hoop off his own miss, 15-footer and another offensive rebound. Washburn sank a free throw during the sequence but the damage was done and so was North Carolina State.

"Manning got loose," North Carolina State's Jim Valvano said. "From there we broke down and it was his game."

N.C. State made one final thrust, closing to 64-62. But Washburn was called for goal-tending a Greg Dreiling layup and Dreiling added a flip hook to make it 68-63.

Dreiling finished with 19 points and 12 rebounds, but it was Manning, with 22 points, who won the game.

"Danny's greatness is versatility for his size," Valvano said. "That's what makes him so difficult to contain, and we couldn't do it."

The 1986 Jayhawks finished a 35-4, setting a school record for victories, and reached the Final Four. Seated (L-R): Archie Marshall, Jerry Johnson, Mark Pellock, Danny Manning, Greg Dreiling, Rodney Hull, Chris Piper, Calvin Thompson. Standing (L-R): manager Bill Pope, manager Kurt Unruh, Cedric Hunter, Jeff Johnson, Ron Kellogg, Milt Newton, Scooter Barry, Mark Turgeon, Altonio Campbell, manager Donnell Martin.

Kansas makes international statement
Nov. 19, 1986

Lawrence - The Soviet Union won two of the three Olympic gold medals in the 1980s. So when the red-clad Russians came to your gym, it was no ordinary exhibition game.

The 1986 Soviets included several Olympians and one Sarunas Marcilenus, who went on to succeed in the NBA. The team wasn't unbeatable, it had lost four college games on a tour that would end in Lawrence. But the outcome that had gained the Jayhawks' attention was a 28-point victory over Oklahoma.

A crowd of 15,400 wanted to see how Kansas would measure up against one of the world's best amateur teams. They weren't disappointed. The Soviets pushed the early pace and lead 39-38 at the break.

Mark Turgeon provided the second-half spark. He scored 15 of his 17 after the break, including five straight to break a 47-47 tie. From there, Kansas, which was starting its season, took advantage of the Russians' tired legs. The lead swelled to 80-57.

The game was something of a coming-out party for Turgeon, a senior who started for the first time. Turgeon was down on himself for letting his man score toward the end of the half, and Larry Brown wasn't happy either. It was only the preseason but Brown lit into Turgeon for about five minutes.

"I needed to show my leadership to the younger players and I went in and did some stupid things," Turgeon said.

Turgeon's play inspired everybody. Danny Manning finished with 28 and Kevin Pritchard had 12.

The victory didn't count in the record book, and it wasn't officially part of the Jayhawks' 55-game home floor winning streak. But it made some important statements: Kansas could beat the best in the world, and Turgeon could play the point.

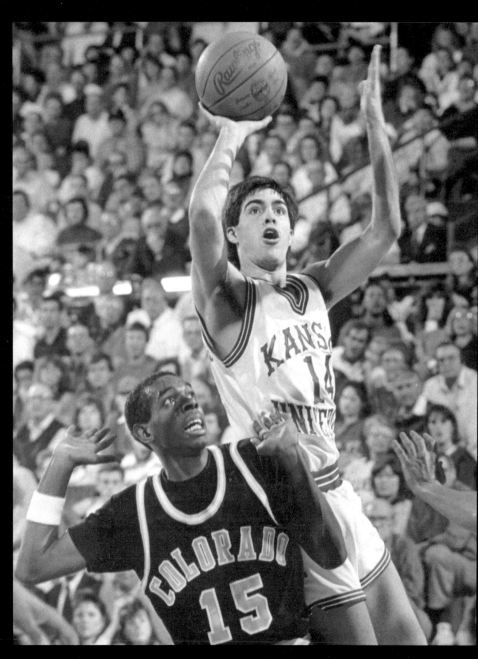

Kevin Pritchard.

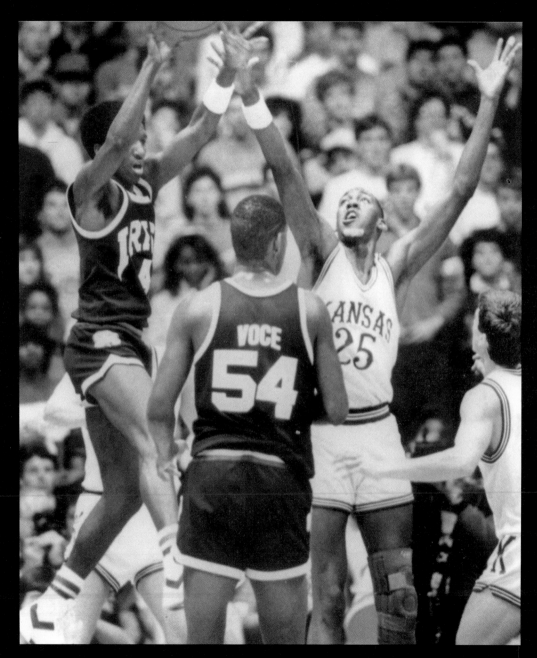

Danny Manning battles Notre Dame's David Rivers.

Irish eyes aren't smiling
Feb. 8, 1987

Lawrence - Even in basketball, Notre Dame carries a mystique. When the Irish visited Kansas for the first time in 12 years, they also carried a giant-slayer reputation.

A week earlier, Notre Dame had knocked off No. 1 North Carolina. The Jayhawks weren't ranked that high, but there was a striking similarity in the Irish opponents. The Tar Heels played without injured star point guard Kenny Smith. Kansas was without its starting point guard, Cedric Hunter, who had suffered a sprained ankle the day before in a victory over Oklahoma State.

That meant Mark Turgeon, who had started five games earlier in the season, had to fill in. Danny Manning made it easy on everybody.

Manning finished with a career-high 40 points. No other Kansas player had more than eight.

"I've seen him play great for 30 minutes, but I've never seen him play great for 38 minutes like that," Larry Brown said. "Offensively, it was the best I've ever seen him."

Manning went 16 for 21 from the field and eight of 11 from the line. With 1:42 remaining and the Jayhawks clinging to a two-point lead, Turgeon fired a pass to Manning on the baseline. He flipped it in and was fouled. After the Irish hit a free throw, Turgeon and Manning delivered again. Manning hit from 15, and the game was over.

"I knew I had to score today," Manning said. "I didn't know how much I had to score. But I knew I had to pick it up in Ced's absence. I told him before the game that we'd be all right and this one was going to be for him."

Turgeon finished with nine assists, but his defensive work on David Rivers was more important. Rivers finished with 13 and made only three of eight from the floor.

"I woke up last night and it was hard to get back to sleep," Turgeon said. "I was thinking about David Rivers. But I didn't feel any pressure. I've played in big games before."

New lineup leads way
Feb. 10, 1988

Stillwater, Okla. -

Four straight losses had dropped Kansas to 12-8 and even after a home victory over Colorado, something needed to change. Larry Brown shuffled the lineup.

Slumping Lincoln Minor went to the bench and in his place went sophomore Jeff Gueldner.

"Physically, he's OK," Brown said. "He just doesn't deserve to play right now."

It may have had something to do with a streak of 15 straight misses on three-pointers.

Gueldner knocked in a three-pointer to open the scoring against the Cowboys. It was his only field goal of the game, but the Jayhawks turned in one of their more solid efforts of the season. They shot 61.5 percent from the floor and made all six from behind the arc.

Danny Manning had 23 and Kevin Pritchard came up big with 20 points and six assists.

"I felt OK about the job we did with Manning," Oklahoma State coach Leonard Hamilton said. "Where we broke down was Pritchard. He had an almost perfect night. The only thing he didn't do was sell popcorn."

Cowboys forward Richard Dumas missed 11 of 12 from the field. Guard John Starks was the only Oklahoma State starter with more than one field goal.

Kansas made 10 of 11 from the line in the final four minutes to keep a safe lead.

The Jayhawks had hit on the right combination - Manning, Pritchard, Milt Newton, Chris Piper and now Gueldner. The new lineup would stay intact for the rest of the season, one that would last longer than anybody expected.

Kansas 64, Kansas State 63

A final strike in Ahearn
Feb. 18, 1988

Manhattan – Kansas' final visit to Ahearn Field House, the Kansas State home since 1951, went down to the wire, and somebody besides Danny Manning won it for the Jayhawks.

A big shot from Kevin Pritchard, plus Milt Newton's defense on Wildcats star Mitch Richmond paved the way and extended KU's winning streak to five.

Pritchard's three-pointer with 29 seconds left broke a 61-61 deadlock. Richmond hit a baseline jumper with 14 seconds remaining, then Kansas left the door open when Keith Harris missed two free throws with four seconds to play.

K-State got a timeout and had three seconds to get something. But long pass from Charles Bledsoe to midcourt flew over Richmond's head and into the hands of Wildcats' Fred McCoy, who lost control of the ball as the buzzer sounded.

Kansas got revenge on the team that ended its 55-game homecourt winning streak three weeks earlier. In that game, Richmond scored 35.

This time, Richmond made four of 17 from the field and finished with 11. The field goal with 14 seconds left was his only one of the second half. Newton, for the most part, and Harris did the job.

"I've had more frustrating games but that doesn't make this one any easier," Richmond said.

The loss to KU in Manhattan the previous year was just as tough, said Richmond. He went four of 20 in a double-overtime loss.

Kansas 85, Xavier 72

KU tops Xavier in opening act
March 18, 1988

Lincoln, Neb. – Would Kansas be ready for the NCAA Tournament? The answer came in the opening minutes of the first-round encounter with Xavier.

The Jayhawks, seeded sixth, roared to a 48-29 halftime lead over a team that averaged nearly 100 points per game.

"We were outclassed," Musketeers coach Pete Gillen said. "They were very aggressive. They came out with fire. They scratched, clawed, got all the loose balls. And you can't get behind to a team that has the greatest player in America."

That would be Danny Manning, who did his part with 24 points. Milt Newton added 21 and each grabbed 12 rebounds.

Kansas entered the game with some trepidation. Starting guard Kevin Pritchard had injured his knee in the Big Eight Tournament and his status was uncertain. Larry Brown said he'd probably go with Clint Normore. But Pritchard went through pre-game warm-ups with little problem and got the starting call.

Also, Xavier was a scary first-round foe. The Musketeers were well coached. They had knocked off Missouri in an opening round game the previous year. Because of their scoring ability they had been compared to Oklahoma, which had defeated Kansas twice during the regular season. Their top player, Byron Larkin, figured to create matchup problems.

But Larkin was hardly a factor. He finished with 16 but made only six of 18 from the floor. Xavier shot 37.5 percent from the floor, to the Jayhawks' 54.7 percent.

We probably played as well in the first half as any time during the year," Brown said.

Kevin Pritchard gains control against Murray State in the 1988 NCAA Tournament.

Kansas survives by overcoming last minute deficit
March 20, 1988

Lincoln, Neb. - The upset opportunity was supposed to come in the first game. Xavier is always pulling off those kinds of victories.

But the Jayhawks' second-round opponent, lowly Murray State of the Ohio Valley Conference, nearly came up with a second straight shocker. The Racers had knocked out third seed North Carolina State two days earlier.

Now, with 50 seconds remaining against Kansas, Murray State's Jeff Martin nailed two free throws for a 58-57 lead. But a lob pass from Scooter Barry to Danny Manning turned into a Manning 8-foot jump hook restored the KU lead with 37 seconds left.

Murray State played for the victory. Don Mann's 10-foot jumper with three seconds remaining missed. Manning grabbed the rebound, was fouled and made both free throws with one tick left for the final margin.

"I look at the last minute of the game and it typifies our season," Larry Brown said. "Danny makes the shot to go ahead, gets the big rebound, makes the free throws. I've been on his case all year about rebounding and he got the biggest rebound of the year for us as far as I'm concerned."

Manning finished with 25 and scored eight of the Jayhawks' final 10. But it had been a frustrating afternoon. The Racers played a sagging 2-3 zone, attempting to keep the ball from Manning.

That meant others had to step up. Kevin Pritchard finished with 16 and played a key role in the second half. He scored eight straight points that allowed Kansas to turn a 34-32 deficit into a six-point lead.

But the final minute belonged to Manning, who ran his tournament total to 49 points and 17 rebounds. When the regular-season ended and honor ballots were counted, Manning wasn't a unanimous call for national player of the year. Bradley's Hersey Hawkins won the award from the wire services and the United States Basketball Writers Association. Manning won the Wooden and Naismith awards.

A week into the NCAA Tournament, Hawkins team didn't get out of the first round, and Manning was carrying his team to the Sweet 16.

Win over Vandy is dandy
March 25, 1988

Pontiac, Mich. - No NCAA Tournament is complete without a spate of upsets. In 1988, most were happening in the Midwest, and Kansas was the beneficiary.

The Jayhawks had reached the Sweet 16 by beating 11th-seeded Xavier and 14th-seeded Murray State. Next was seventh-seeded Vanderbilt, which had defeated No. 2 Pittsburgh.

The Commodores were led by center Will Perdue. Kansas didn't have a 7-foot body to match up, so it played a team defense. Guards applied pressure out front, limiting entry passes, big men fronted him, keeping him from catching the ball low.

Instead of scoring inside, Vanderbilt looked outside. It shot 20 three-pointers, making eight. But the lack of inside muscle was the difference.

Perdue finished with 16, two below his average. He scored his first basket four minutes into the game and didn't attempt another shot for six more minutes. By then, Kansas had a 21-8 lead. The advantage was 12 at halftime and 15 midway through the second half.

But Vandy inched back. Kansas scored only one point over a three-minute stretch and the margin was down to 60-51.

The Jayhawks caught their breath and pulled away. Again, Danny Manning showed the way. His basket had restored the double-digit lead adding to his 38 points. Opposing coaches were starting to sound like a broken record.

"We got beat by a team that was very well prepared and by a great player who had one of the better games I've ever seen," Vandy's C.M. Newton said. "Manning was nearly unstoppable."

The player charged with trying was Frank Kornet. But while Kornet may have been present in spirit, his body couldn't keep up.

"I tried to make him stay out on the floor and shoot the turnaround jumper," Kornet said. "But he has such a quick turnaround there was nothing I could do but just try to get a hand in his face.

"I could see in his face he felt like everything he shot was going in, and it did. It was like 'When is this guy going to miss?' I guess he showed why he's the player of the year."

Final Four reward for Sunflower victory
Mar. 27, 1988

Pontiac, Mich. - The eyes of a nation were cast upon state rivals who faced each other for the fourth time in a season. Kansas vs. Kansas State, with a Final Four spot in Kansas City for the winner.

The Wildcats, seeded fourth, had knocked off top-seeded Purdue, to reach the final. The path was easier for sixth-seeded Kansas. No. 3 North Carolina State and No. 2 Pittsburgh were upset. The Wildcats were the best team KU faced in four tournament games.

K-State had won two of three, including a 69-54 triumph in the semifinals of the Big Eight Tournament. But the regional game more closely resembled the Jayhawks' triumph in Manhattan.

Mitch Richmond, who was held to a season low 11 at K-State, hit that figure again. He was suffocated by Milt Newton, who finished with 18 points, nine rebounds and seven assists.

That was the key. Kansas State had taken a 34-27 lead early in the second half, and if Richmond had ever found the range perhaps the Wildcats could have run away. Instead, the Jayhawks clawed back. Richmond committed two turnovers in a two-minute stretch and Kansas converted both into baskets and a 49-44 lead.

K-State had lost its poise and Kansas was getting contributions from everybody. Scooter Barry finished with a career-high 15. Lincoln Minor and Keith Harris came up with three steals between them to fuel the rally. Danny Manning scored 20 and was the regional MVP, but this was more of a team effort.

"We know what Danny is going to do," Larry Brown said. "We just got some great performances from the other kids. I'm amazed at Milt's line."

Newton was terrific, especially on defense, and joined Manning on the all-regional team. The Jayhawks were headed to their second Final Four in three years.

"We had everything going for us today," Brown said. "Emotionally, it was on our side. There was a lot of pressure on K-State. They're supposed to beat us. They were convinced they could beat us, and they did beat us pretty good in the Big Eight Tournament. But can you believe it? We're going to Kansas City."

Kevin Pritchard collides with Duke's Phil Henderson in the 1988 NCAA semifinal.

Fast start finishes Duke
April 2, 1988

Kansas City - If

Kansas owed anybody it was Duke.

The Blue Devils had defeated the Jayhawks in the 1986 national semifinals when Kansas believed it was the better team. Duke also had beaten the Jayhawks earlier that the season for the Preseason NIT crown, and six weeks before the 1988 Final Four encounter at Kemper Arena the Blue Devils had captured an overtime decision in Lawrence.

Kansas was pumped from the start. Chris Piper dropped in two free throws, Milt Newton tossed in a three-pointer and Danny Manning added two baskets for a 9-0 lead before Duke took a time out with 16:26 left. Newton then banged in another three-pointer for a 12-0 lead. Kansas had come up with three steals on Duke's first four possessions.

"We came out very tentative and you can't just come out and dig yourself in a hole like that," Duke forward Danny Ferry said.

But the hole grew deeper. It was 18-2 after Manning converted a three-point play. A few minutes later,

Milt Newton launches a jumper in the Jayhawks' victory over Duke in the 1988 semifinals.

Kansas had its largest lead at 24-6.

The Blue Devils settled down and closed to 38-27 at halftime. But another strong KU surge at the beginning of the second half returned an 18-point margin. The Blue Devils chipped away. It was 51-44 with 11 minutes remaining, then 55-52 with four minutes to play.

Piper hit a pair of free throws for a 61-55 lead with 1:43 left and the game was on ice.

"All the great teams make runs at you and they made theirs," Manning said. "The same thing happened in Lawrence, and we learned from that."

In the regular-season game, KU led 23-8 and lost by four in overtime. Manning wasn't going to let Kansas lose this one. He finished with 25 points and 10 rebounds. Newton added 20 and Piper 10.

The Jayhawks had wiped out all the sour tastes left by the Blue Devils and were in the title game for the first time since 1957.

Lincoln Minor and Jeff Gueldner embrace as the final seconds tick away in the 1988 championship game.

Danny and the Miracles
Apr. 4, 1988

Kansas City - Championship game upsets marked the NCAA Tournament in the 1980s and several key elements were common to victories by North Carolina State in 1983, Villanova in 1985 and Kansas in 1988.

All met a conference opponent late in the bracket that had swept the regular-season series: N.C. State beat Virginia in the West Regional finals, Villanova defeated Georgetown for the title and Kansas beat Oklahoma in the final. Heavy underdogs weren't going to be intimidated by a familiar foe. In these championship games, all underdogs made early statements. Any inclination by the favorites to take their opponent lightly was eliminated quickly.

And all three were brilliantly coached, but strategies differed. In a period before the shot clock, N.C. State's Jim Valvano and Villanova's Rollie Massimino slowed their games considerably.

Kansas' Larry Brown startled the Sooners by playing their game from the opening tip. All season, nobody kept up with Oklahoma, which averaged 102.9 points per game. But the Jayhawks opened in a dead sprint and produced perhaps the most entertaining half of a championship game. It was 50-50 at the break. KU had shot 71 percent.

"I don't think they could have shot it any better," Oklahoma coach Billy Tubbs said. "Maybe our defense was lacking. We never had a firm control of this game."

Brown's strategy was the reason. The other big difference between Kansas and the other upset winners was Danny Manning. The Wolfpack and Wildcats won without a national player of the year caliber force. The Jayhawks couldn't have won without theirs.

Manning's 31-point, 18-rebound night is one of the greatest in title game history. He was every bit as important to the Jayhawks' victory as Bill Walton was to UCLA's when he scored 44 in 1973 or Jack Givens to Kentucky's when he scored 41 in 1978.

"Whenever they needed a basket they went to their big man," Oklahoma's Harvey Grant said. "That's how they won."

No doubt everybody for Kansas raised their game a notch against the Sooners. Milt Newton's defense, Clint Normore coming up with seven first-half points, Lincoln Minor with four points, Scooter Barry, Kevin Pritchard, Jeff Gueldner all played well. But when Manning elevated his game, the Jayhawks felt unbeatable.

Manning came up big in the final minute, not with anything spectacular but just solid play and hustle. Mookie Blaylock cut the KU lead to 78-77 with a jumper and Kansas spread its offense. Barry went to the free throw line where he made the first and missed the second. Manning ran down the rebound and was fouled. Then he made two free throws.

After a Ricky Grace basket, Manning buried two more with five seconds left to clinch the game.

Like N.C. State and Villanova, Kansas had pulled off the improbable. So often the Jayhawks have lost in the tournament when it believed it had the best team or was given a terrific opportunity to win: 1953, 1957, 1966 and 1986 come to mind. And after Brown and Manning departed there were gut-wrenching losses in 1990, 1992, 1996 and 1997.

But 1988 will be remembered as the year Kansas got supreme coaching and clutch shooting in the final and captured a tournament it had no business winning. The victory in Kansas City, dubbed Danny and the Miracles, stands as the greatest moment in the program's history.

The 1988 national champions at the Memorial Stadium ceremony

Boxscore of 1988 NCAA championship game

KANSAS

	MP	FG-A	FT-A	R	A	F	TP
Milt Newton	32	6-6	1-2	4	1	1	15
Chris Piper	37	4-6	0-0	7	2	3	8
D. Manning	36	13-24	5-7	18	2	3	31
K. Pritchard	31	6	70-0	1	4	1	13
J. Gueldner	15	1-2	0-0	2	1	0	2
Scooter Barry	9	0-2	1-2	0	2	1	1
Clint Normore	16	3-3	0-1	1	4	3	7
Keith Harris	13	1-1	0-0	1	0	2	2
Lincoln Minor	11	1-4	2-2	1	1	1	4
Mike Maddox	1	0-0	0-0	0	0	1	0
Totals	200	35-55	9-14	36	17	16	83

Three-pointers: Newton 2-2, Manning 0-1, Pritchard 1-1, Gueldner 0-1, Normore 1-1. Total 4-6.

Turnovers: Piper 5, Prichard 5, Manning 4, Harris 4, Barry 2, Normore 2, Minor 1. Total 23.

Blocked shots: Newton 2, Manning 2.

Steals: Piper 3, Manning 5, Pritchard 1, Gueldner 1, Minor 1, Total 11.

OKLAHOMA

	MP	FG-A	FT-A	R	A	F	TP
Harvey Grant	40	6-14	2-3	5	1	4	14
Dave Sieger	40	7-15	1-2	5	7	2	22
Stacey King	39	7-14	3-3	7	0	3	17
M. Blaylock	40	6-13	0-1	5	4	4	14
Ricky Grace	34	4-14	3-4	7	7	4	12
T. Mullins	7	0-0	0-0	1	0	1	0
Totals	30-70	9-13	9-13	31	19	18	79

Three-pointers: Sieger 7-13, Blaylock 2-4, Grace 1-7. Total 10-14.

Turnovers: Sieger 6, King 3, Blaylock 2, Grace 3, Mullins 1. Total 15.

Blocked shots: King 2, Grant 1. Total 3.

Steals: Blaylock 7, Sieger 3, Grant 1, Grace 1, King 1.

Halftime: 50-50

Officials: John Clougherty, Tim Higgins, Ed Hightower.

Attendance: 16,392.

Ronald Reagan accepts a Kansas letter jacket from Danny Manning
at the White House ceremony after the 1988 championship.

KU fans line Mass Street for 1988 championship team parade.

1988 NCAA championship game play-by-play

First half

Time remaining		KU-OU
19:54	Blaylock 19-foot jumper	0-2
19:24	Manning 13-foot jumper	2-2
19:14	Manning 10-foot hook	4-2
18:44	King 12-foot bank	4-4
18:31	Pritchard 10-foot jumper	6-4
17:46	Newton 11-foot jumper	8-4
17:23	Sieger three-pointer	8-7
17:03	Piper follow	10-7
16:20	King 10-foot jumper	10-9
15:40	Grant 7-foot jumper	10-11
15:30	Pritchard 11-foot jumper	12-11
15:09	Manning layup	14-11
14:41	Grant 8-foot turnaround	14-13
14:08	Newton reverse layup	16-13
13:43	Normore layup	18-13
13:07	King layup and FT	18-16
12:56	Manning slam from Barry lob	20-16
12:04	Sieger three-pointer	20-19
11:49	Manning layup	22-19
11:22	Normore layup	24-19
11:11	King 12-foot jumper	24-21
11:03	Gueldner layup	26-21
10:43	King 2 FTs	26-23
10:30	Harris 10-foot jumper	28-23
10:16	Blaylock 6-foot follow	28-25
10:05	Pritchard three-pointer	31-25
9:27	Sieger three-pointer	31-28
8:59	King 6-foot jumper	31-30
8:52	Newton 16-foot jumper	33-30
8:39	Blaylock three-pointer	33-33
7:40	Normore three-pointer	36-33
7:16	Grant 2 FTs	36-35
6:32	Grant 10-foot jumper	36-37
5:40	King slam	36-39
5:17	Manning 10-foot jumper	38-39
5:12	Minor 2 FTs	40-39
4:54	Sieger three-pointer	40-42
4:37	Newton three-pointer	43-42
4:03	Sieger three-pointer	43-45
3:22	Minor 15-footer	45-45
1:44	Sieger three-pointer	45-48
:59	Newton three-pointer	48-48
:44	Manning layup	50-48
:22	Grace 7-foot jumper	50-50

First half statistics

	KU	OU
FG-A	22-31	19-39
FG%	71.0	48.7
FT-A	2-3	5-7
FT%	66.7	63.6
3PT	4-5	7-11
3PT%	80.0	71.4
Reb	15	17
Turn	15	11
Fouls	19	6

Scoring leaders
Kansas: Manning 14
Oklahoma: Sieger 18

Second half

19:44	Grant 12-foot jumper	50-52
19:03	Pritchard layup	52-52
18:02	Manning layup	54-52
17:48	King 11-foot jumper	54-54
17:19	Newton 17-foot jumper	56-54
16:32	Manning 10-footer	58-54
15:16	Grace three-pointer	58-57
14:14	Pritchard 16-footer	60-57
14:03	Grace FT	60-58
13:26	Sieger three-pointer	60-61
13:12	Blaylock layup	60-63
12:13	King 6-footer	60-65
11:53	Piper 16-footer	62-65
11:13	Manning inside and FT	65-65
11:01	Blaylock three-pointer	65-68
10:20	Manning layup	67-68
8:51	Manning layup	69-68
7:38	Piper 16-footer	71-68
6:55	Sieger FT	71-69
6:13	Grant 13-foot jumper	71-71
5:35	Pritchard 10-foot jumper	73-71
4:26	Manning inside	75-71
3:05	Piper 8-foot jumper	77-71
2:02	Grace 2 FTs	77-73
1:13	Newton FT	78-73
:59	Grace layup	78-75
:41	Blaylock 13-foot jumper	78-77
:16	Barry FT	79-77
:10	Manning 2 FTs	81-77
:09	Grace layup	81-79
:05	Manning 2 FTs	83-79

Comments
Larry Brown

"This is something that about two months ago was totally unexpected. When it was 50-50 at halftime, and we were shooting 70 percent, we were concerned because we couldn't get ourselves slowed down. We were just hoping to get it to the last five minutes."

Danny Manning

"This feels great to be able to close out my career like this, in Kansas City, in front of people that have cheered me and supported me for four years. It's a great feeling and something we deserved. This wasn't a gift."

Billy Tubbs

"It's a bitter defeat because we thought we could win it all. We didn't and we have to accept that."

Notes

The game was tied 11 times and there were 13 lead changes.

Kansas' 11 losses are the most for a team that won the NCAA championship.

Oklahoma became the first team to play for the football and basketball championship in the same year. It lost both.

The 100 points in the first half was a championship game record.

Roy Williams

Seasons (1988-Present)
Conference championships: 1991, 1992, 1993, 1995, 1996, 1997
Homecourt: Allen Field House (16,300)

Kansas fans were in for a shock when Larry Brown's successor was identified. Athletic director Bob Frederick had his pick of worthy candidates like Ohio State's Gary Williams and Southwest Missouri State's Charlie Spoonhour.

Instead, the call went to Roy Williams, a fulltime North Carolina assistant for the previous four seasons. Kansas had just won a national championship with a Carolina grad, but this was different. Nobody outside of Chapel Hill had heard of Williams.

It didn't take long for Williams to make an impression. Kansas lost to Seton Hall in the title game of the Great Alaska Shootout, then won 11 straight to climb into the national rankings. The first team finished 19-12 and would have made the NCAA Tournament if not for probation.

The next season, Kansas was picked to finish sixth in the Big Eight preseason poll. A 19-0 start, including victories over No. 2 LSU and No. 1 UNLV in the Preseason NIT, propelled the Jayhawks to No. 1.

A year later, Kansas played for the NCAA championship. Two seasons later, another Final Four appearance.

Kansas hasn't been back to the Final Four since 1993, but the decade has produced the longest period of sustained high-level success in the program's history. Kansas is college basketball's winningest program of the decade. The Jayhawks weren't even in the top 10 of winningest programs (by percentage) in the 1980s, 1970s, 1960s, 1950s or 1940s

Only the Jayhawks have reached the Sweet 16 of the NCAA Tournament in each of the past five years, and only KU has been ranked first for at least one week in each of the past five years.

Williams has won more games in the first nine years as a head coach than anybody who's coached at the major college level. His winning percentage (.805) is the second highest among active coaches.

A major reason for Williams' success is the program's ability to buck a trend and keep its top underclassmen in school. Jacque Vaughn decided to return for his senior year. Junior Raef LaFrentz and sophomore Paul Pierce made the same choice. Nearly every other major program has lost a standout before his eligibility has expired.

The toughest NCAA tournament loss may have been in 1997. The Jayhawks were the tournament's No. 1 seed for the first time and lost to Arizona in the Sweet 16. Otherwise, Williams' success is incomparable. Interest in the program is at an all-time high. Every home game sells out.

1989-90 starting five: L-R Pekka Markkanen, Rick Calloway, Jeff Gueldner, Mark Randall and Kevin Pritchard.

League debut is blowout
Jan. 7, 1989

Lawrence – Kansas invited its former letter-winners to see the opening Big Eight game in Roy Williams' tenure and the Jayhawks couldn't have provided a better show.

Before 80 former players, Kansas ran up record totals against the Cyclones. The 127 points and 71 in the second half were all-time bests.

"When people around the country see this score they'll think the roof caved in on them or something," Williams said.

Nine players scored in double figures, led by Mark Randall's 18. Kansas went 44 for 77 from the floor (57.1 percent) and made seven of 12 three-pointers.

Kansas led 19-4 to open the game, but Iowa State cut it to 12 at halftime. Fewer than two minutes into the second half, the margin was nine. Then the Jayhawks pressed the accelerator, outscoring the Cyclones 67-31 the rest of the way to claim their 10th straight victory.

"That team is better than any Kansas team I've played before," Iowa State coach Johnny Orr said. "They were terrific."

It was a night to think of what might be. Kansas, serving a year a NCAA probation and unable to defend its NCAA Tournament championship, looked like a sure postseason participant against Iowa State.

"It would make my day if during the tournament television announcers would say 'I wonder what would happen if Kansas was here?' " Kevin Pritchard said.

Mark Randall

Shaq attacked
Nov, 17, 1989

Baton Rouge, La. - This was only the
second round and four victories were needed to capture the
Preseason NIT. So how did LSU coach Dale Brown know?

"You just saw, probably, the NIT champion tonight," Brown
said. "I seriously doubt anybody will beat Kansas in New
York."

Few gave the Jayhawks a chance to beat the second-ranked
Tigers, loaded with players like Shaquille O'Neal, Chris
Jackson and Stanley Roberts. But Kansas won, convincingly
to Brown, and it did it while making only 11 of 24 from the
free-throw line.

Kevin Pritchard made one when it counted. He dropped in
a free throw with 23 seconds remaining that gave the
Jayhawks an 87-83 edge. LSU didn't have the ball again
with a chance to tie.

O'Neal, playing in his second game for the Tigers, was
schooled by Mark Randall, Pekka Markkanen and Mike
Maddox off the bench. On offense, Randall stayed away
from the basket and scored most of his 26 from the perime-
ter. That brought O'Neal away from the basket, which
explained his 10 points and seven rebounds. O'Neal fouled
out with 3:42 remaining.

The real problem was Jackson, who had set an NCAA
freshman scoring record the previous year with a 30.2 average. Nobody could match Jackson's quickness, but the
Jayhawks succeeded in not allowing Jackson to fake and
drive. Jackson took too many jumpers. He scored 32 but was
11 for 30 from the floor, four for 17 in the second half.

"You're never going to shut down Chris Jackson," Pritchard
said. "You've got to try and take away his easy shots. He's
quick and good, but I don't know if he can play much worse
than he did tonight."

The game turned in the first half. LSU led 23-16, but the
Jayhawks used a 19-6 run over the next six minutes. Terry
Brown popped in four of five from behind the line during
the stretch. The shocking upset that Roy Williams later
called "the first big-time win" in his head coaching career
was on.

"For this time of year," Rick Calloway said, "it was nearly
perfect."

Kansas stuns No. 1 Rebels
Nov. 22, 1989

New York - Beating LSU was one thing. Playing Nevada-Las Vegas in the Preseason NIT semifinal figured to provide a stiffer challenge. These were the No. 1 Runnin' Rebels of Larry Johnson and Stacey Augmon.

When UNLV raced to a 36-28 lead, the Rebels seemed to have Kansas on the run. But in a flash, the Jayhawks assumed control. Jeff Gueldner's jumper and a three-pointer by Adonis Jordan got things rolling. Two Mark Randall free throws and another trey by Jordan gave Kansas the lead.

From there, it was all KU. The second-half lead soared to 83-63. The Rebels couldn't solve the Kansas running game, backdoor passes or halfcourt trap.

Adonis Jordan.

Randall and center Pekka Markkanen double-teammed Johnson most of the night and the highly regarded junior college transfer finished with 13

Mike Maddox came off the bench for Kansas and scored 17. Markkanen, coming off a scoreless game at LSU, finished with 14.

"We caught them on a good night," Roy Williams said. "They just didn't play well."

Maybe. But Kansas was fantastic. Anybody who believed the LSU victory was a fluke knew better now. In a five-day span, the Jayhawks had defeated the nation's Nos. 2 and 1 ranked teams.

"To beat the No. 1 and No. 2 teams, you've got to have something," guard Kevin Prtitchard said. "You don't just get lucky when you do that."

NIT crown caps spectacular tournament
Nov. 25, 1989

New York - A few years after winning the 1989 Preseason NIT, Roy Williams was playing a round of golf, some sort of corporate function, and was teamed with an ESPN executive, oblivious to his partner's occupation.

"He said he remembered the year the NIT could have had UNLV and LSU in New York, along with St. John's, but this team he couldn't remember messed up everything," Williams said. "I told him I coached the team that messed it up."

The Jayhawks still had some work to do after their breathtaking victories over LSU and UNLV to reach the NIT final. No. 25 St. John's was the opponent and the home favorite.

But Kansas wasn't about to come this far and lose. The Jayhawks had dictated a fast tempo in the previous NIT games, including a 109-83 blowout of Alabama-Birmingham in the opener. The Redmen wanted to slow the pace. Didn't matter. KU led by 13 at the break.

For the first time in the tournament, the Jayhawks were pushed hard in the second half. St. John's came back to take a one-point lead with six minutes remaining. But Kansas outscored the Redmen 11-1 to end the game.

"I thought that was good for us," Roy Williams said. "I wanted to see what the heck we were made of."

Apparently more than voters in the poll thought a few weeks earlier. Kansas got no votes in the preseason poll and was picked to finish anywhere from sixth to eighth in the Big Eight. Now, the Jayhawks had defeated three straight ranked teams. They jumped from nowhere to No. 4.

"We honestly didn't know what kind of team we had," said guard Kevin Pritchard. "But I think people underestimated our talent. We've got talent, and I think people are starting to realize that now. You don't win this tournament without talent."

Or confidence.

"This team is confident," said Mark Randall, the tournament's most valuable player. "Confident that we can play with anybody in the country."

The Jayhawks set a bushel of scoring records in a 150-95 romp over Kentucky.
Guard Terry Brown came off the bench to lead KU with 31 points.

Record win for Kansas, loss for Kentucky
Dec. 9, 1989

Lawrence - With Christmas approaching, Roy Williams received plenty of mail from Kentucky. They weren't seasons greetings.

Fans of the Kentucky Wildcats were fuming days after absorbing the biggest defeat in the program's modern era. The 150 points were the most scored by Kansas and against a Kentucky team.

"I'm going to answer them," Williams said. "I'm going to be as honest as I possibly can and say I had no intentions of it being that kind of score.

"I am going to say I made a mistake, and I don't mind admitting it. Looking back on it, I think about the 6- or 7-minute mark we had tired signals from three players, and I probably should have put in those last three guys."

Those guys were Macolm Nash, Todd Alexander and Kirk Wagner, and they entered the game with 3:31 remaining. The Jayhawks led 141-90 at the time.

"Outside of the NCAA Tournament, that's probably the most fun I've had here," senior guard Kevin Pritchard said.

Kentucky was making it fun for Kansas. The Wildcats entered the game with several handicaps. Probation had limited the number of scholarship players to eight, and they had nobody taller than 6-7. Kentucky entered the game with a 3-1 record and were doing little more than bombing in three-pointers and pressing.

The Wildcats went on to lead the nation in three-pointers per game at 10.04 and set an NCAA record by averaging 28.9 attempts per game from behind the arc. On this day -

Official Ed Hightower slaps Kentucky coach Rick Pitino with a technical foul.

Kentucky attempted 40 treys - the strategy was death.

Kansas was rarely rattled by the pressure. The Jayhawks had seven turnovers in the first half and led 80-61, a school record for points in a half.

Terry Brown scored 31 points in 19 minutes. Starting forward Mark Randall played 28 minutes. The other starters played between 14-26 minutes. No matter who was in the game, neither side retreated from its game plan: Kentucky pressed and Kansas attacked.

To reporters, first-year Kentucky coach Rick Pitino didn't complain. "I have no problem with what happened," Pitino said. "It would have been embarrassing if Kansas didn't try to score, if they came down and didn't shoot. I would have been upset by that."

A year later, Kentucky got a measure of revenge. The Wildcats defeated Kansas in Lexington, Ky., 88-71.

Hoosiers ambushed
March 21, 1991

Charlotte, N.C. - Five minutes into the Southeast Regional semifinal, the game was stopped as the officials looked at a problem with the floor. Indiana coach Bob Knight strolled over and suggested the game be started from scratch.

Considering Kansas started the game with a 26-6 lead, Knight couldn't be blamed.

"'I've said many times that this team may not be the prettiest, but tonight may have been one of the prettiest games I've ever seen," Roy Williams said.

The Jayhawks were unstoppable. Guard Terry Brown knocked down three from behind the arc in the first four minutes.

"I was very disappointed in our start," Knight said. "We were too tentative. Kansas was very aggressive."

Kansas led by 20 eight minutes into the game. The Jayhawks didn't shoot lights out - 45.9 percent from the floor for the night - but they cut up Indiana with crisp passing, smothered the Hoosiers with an active defense, dominated the boards and kept mistakes to a minimum.

The Jayhawks had four turnovers in the first half, all on offense fouls. Not once did Kansas throw away a possession.

"I don't remember us playing a better 20 minutes all season," forward Alonzo Jamison said.

Indiana closed to 11 twice in the first half but never cut the margin into single digits after the opening minutes.

The Jayhawks slowed the tempo and protected their lead. Kansas was never threatened and earned a date with Arkansas for the regional championship.

The 1991 Jayhawks played for the NCAA championship. Front row (L-R) assistant coach Steve Robinson, assistant coach Kevin Stallings, assistant coach Mark Turgeon, Kirk Wagner, Mike Maddox, Terry Brown, Mark Randall, head coach Roy Williams, assistant coach Jerry Green, trainer Mark Cairns. Back row (L-R): manager Glenn Boor, manager Dave Van Daff, Sean Tunstall, Doug Elstun, Rex Walters, Richard Scott, Pat Richey, David Johanning, Macolm Nash, Alonzo Jamison, Steve Woodberry, Adonis Jordan, manager Jay Price, manager Matt Wingate, manager Ann Fowler.

Kansas drives Hogs wild
March 23, 1991

Charlotte, N.C. -
Second-ranked Arkansas trotted off
the floor at halftime with a 12
point-lead and a confident swagger.
The final 20 minutes turned their
strut into a limp.

A stunning second half propelled
Kansas to the Final Four. The
Jayhawks used a 22-7 run early in
the half to soar to a 12-point lead.
Forward Alonzo Jamison played the
game of his life and finished with 26
points, nine rebounds and the
Southeast Regional MVP honor.

"That was the best game I've had at
KU," Jamison said.

Jamison was Kansas' answer to the
Razorbacks' 1-3-1 trap and "40 minutes of hell" defense. He went into
the middle and the Jayhawks were
able to get him the ball.

"That more or less gave us a three
on two," Jamison said. "At practice
the day before I was doing exactly
the same thing against our 1-3-1
trap. When I saw Arkansas do it I
guess you could say my mouth
watered a little bit."

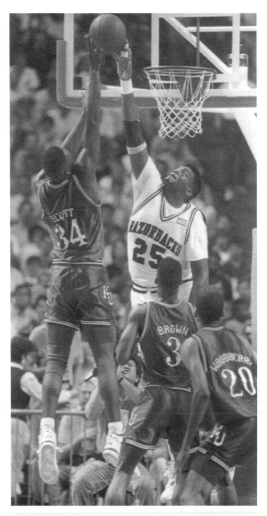

**Richard Scott gets his shot rejected
by Arkansas center Oliver Miller.**

Jamison scored 16 in the second
half, and he also threw a defensive
blanket over Todd Day, who had 21
first-half points. Jamison turned it up
after halftime and Day scored only
five the rest of the way.

"We made him put it on the floor
and went up with him when he
shot," Jamison said. "He was missing
10-foot bank shots. I was loving it.
He really started getting disturbed
with about five minutes left."

The victory capped a remarkable
weekend for the Jayhawks, who
entered the tournament as the
Southeast's third seed. They crushed
third-ranked Indiana and then the
Razorbacks, the only team believed
to have a chance against powerful
Nevada-Las Vegas.

Kansas had conquered Knight and
then defeated Day, and this was
especially satisfying after comments
by Arkansas coach Nolan
Richardson said before the game he
wished the Razorbacks had been
matched against Indiana because a
victory over the Hoosiers would earn
some respect for his program.

Student tops teacher for final
March 30, 1991

Indianapolis - Kansas will never schedule a regular season game against North Carolina as long as Tar Heel grad Roy Williams is coaching the Jayhawks. But a Final Four meeting is acceptable.

Protege met teacher in the national semifinals, and Williams felt so uncomfortable talking about facing Dean Smith he tried not to talk about it the week of the game. But Williams may have wanted to win this game more than any he's coached.

And he did. The mirror image opponents - Williams says 95 percent of what he does he took from North Carolina - played an ugly game. Neither side shot well, and KU three-point marksman Terry Brown went 1 for 10 from the floor.

But Kansas played hard. The Jayhawks won the board battle 51-42, got the loose balls, made the clutch plays.

Kansas began to seize control with 6:20 remaining after North Carolina failed on three tries to erase a one-point deficit. The Jayhawks led 58-57 when Sean Tunstall buried a three-pointer. Richard Scott hit a layup and Adonis Jordan converted a steal for a 7-0 run in 50 seconds.

From there, Kansas made just enough free throws to keep the Tar Heels from having a possession with a chance to at least tie.

"The difference in this game was who wanted it more, and we took it away," forward Mike Maddox said.

It was a tough day for North Carolina seniors Pete Chilcutt, Rick Fox and King Rice - some of whom were recruited by Williams - who combined to make eight of 36 from the floor.

The day also didn't end well for Smith, whose season ended 35 seconds earlier than the rest of the Tar Heels. Smith was called for a second technical foul by official Pete Pavia and ejected. Smith was out of the coaching box and said he was asking Pavia how long he had to make a substitution. Pavia answered with the technical.

"It was embarrassing and I think ridiculous," Smith said.

As Smith exited, he shook hands with Williams and the KU players.

"I always congratulate the other players when the game is over," Smith said. "Well, my game was over."

Kansas athletic director
Bob Frederick
on finding Brown's replacement

❝I offered the job to Dean Smith, but I knew he'd turn it down. It would be hard to leave a place where they just named the arena after him. He suggested an assistant coach of his.❞

Kansas forward Alonzo Jamison found his way to the ball despite a hit by Oklahoma's Angelo Hamilton and despite the presence of Oklahoma's Damon Patterson.

Finally, a victory at Norman
Feb. 2, 1992

Norman, Okla. - In his first three years at Kansas, no team gave Roy Williams more trouble than Oklahoma.

There had been victory and some other close calls. But entering the teams' first meeting in 1992, Billy Tubbs' Sooners owned a 5-2 advantage over Williams-coached teams, and Williams had not won a game at Lloyd Noble Center. Going back to the Larry Brown-era, it had been five straight losses for Kansas in Norman.

The Jayhawks were well on their way to smashing the streak. The lead was 66-48 with 14:44 to play. Oklahoma then outscored Kansas 16-2 over the next four minutes. Center Brian Sallier, with 15 of his 29 in the second half and guard Brent Price with 12 of his 15 after the break led the charge.

But Kansas held firm. Rex Walters buried a three-pointer for a six-point lead with 2:09 left. His sharp pass to Steve Woodberry for a layup kept the margin at six with 1:28 remaining.

The Jayhawks finally could breath easily when Alonzo Jamison scored inside with 10 sec-

onds remaining for a 96-92 edge. A three-pointer just before the buzzer provided the final score, but as the ball was in the air, Williams was off the bench clenching his fist. He knew the Jayhawks couldn't lose.

"We were up 16 and I knew they were going to make the run at us," guard Adonis Jordan said. "It feels great to leave here with a win."

The triumph started a three-game winning streak at Oklahoma for Kansas.

1991-92 starting five: L-R Eric Pauley, Alonzo Jamison, Richard Scott, Rex Walters and Adonis Jordan.

Peeler unstoppable but Tigers fall
March 8, 1992

Lawrence - Anthony Peeler did all he could to foil the Jayhawks' celebration plans.

Kansas had already clinched the Big Eight championship when the Tigers came in for the regular-season finale. But because the title became official earlier in the week, on a night the Jayhawks lost at Iowa State, there had not been a chance to cut the nets.

If the Jayhawks had lost to Missouri the nets would have remained on the rims. The ceremony would have been reduced to seniors accepting the championship trophy from athletic director Bob Frederick.

For most of the afternoon, Kansas was in the clear. It had extended a 53-45 halftime lead into double digits in the final few minutes. Then Peeler warmed up. Swishing three-pointers from all angles he personally kept the Tigers in the game.

Peeler finished with 43, the most against a Roy Williams-coached team (a mark later topped by Jackson State's Lindsey Hunter). He made 16 of 28 from the field and five of nine from behind the arc.

But Kansas, which got double figures scoring from six, broke out the championship hats and T-shirts. Seniors made speeches, and the nets came down.

"I could have lived with the loss because we played very, very well," Williams said. "But I thought it was important for 13 kids to able to stand out there, have the crowd chant, cut down the nets and receive that trophy."

Richard Scott finishes ahead of Missouri's Anthony Peeler.

At home in the dome
Dec. 5, 1992

Indianapolis - Third-ranked Kansas tried
to give the game back to No. 2 Indiana. Rex Walters
wouldn't let it happen.

The Jayhawks went more than nine minutes without a field goal late in the second half, allowing the Hoosiers to turn a six-minute deficit into a three-point lead with 3:26 remaining. The Hoosier Dome crowd of 31,179 - the largest to see Kansas play a regular-season game - was frenetic.

The drought ended with Walters bounced in a short shot on the run with 26 seconds to play, giving KU a 72-69 lead.

"I was hoping to draw in the defense and dump it off," Walters said. "But why risk a bad pass?"

Why, indeed. KU had missed its previous 10 shots. But when the Hoosiers took a 69-66 lead, they didn't score again. Steve Woodberry kept Kansas breathing with four free throws in the next two minutes.

When Damon Bailey missed a three-pointer, preserving a 70-69 KU lead with a minute left, the stage was set for Walters' drive.

"It was fortunate it went in," Walters said. "But a little luck never hurt anything."

Walters and Adonis Jordan each had 16, but it was a horrible shooting day for the Jayhawks. Walters made two of 11 three-pointers and team hit only 40.6 percent on all shots for the day.

Indiana led most of the first half and threatened to pull away before a Kansas rally just before halftime. Richard Scott, who kept KU alive in the first half with 10 points, collected his third foul with 1:13 before half-time.

But Matt Nover missed a free throw, which started a series of mistakes for Indiana. KU scored the final seven points of the half and trailed just 40-38.

"It helped our mental approach and helped them believe what I was trying to tell them at half-time," Roy Williams said.

Rex Walters drives by Damon Bailey in the 1992 KU victory over Indiana at the Hoosier Dome.

Kansas 90, Brigham Young 76

Hot shooting burns BYU
March 20, 1993

Rosemont, Ill. - Rex Walters set the tone for the Jayhawks' 1993 NCAA Tournament run with a record-setting shooting performance in the opening game. Against Ball State, Walters made all six of his three-pointers, tying the tournament record and leading KU to 22-point victory.

The Kansas offense continued to roll against the Cougars. Instead of slowing the pace and playing conservatively KU pulled away by staying aggressive in the final 4:10.

With the Jayhawks leading 70-68, Steve Woodberry nailed a long three-pointer. "I was open, and I have the green light when I'm open," Woodberry said.

The hoop gave Kansas a five-point lead. BYU was called for an offensive foul on the next possession and the Jayhawks never slowed down.

A minute earlier, the Cougars had the momentum. Randy Reid made two free throws to give Brigham Young a 67-66 lead. A defensive hold here and the Cougars would have Kansas on the run.

But Adonis Jordan buried a three-pointer, two minutes after nearly shooting an air ball on the front end of a one-and-one.

"Our offense is about being aggressive," Jordan said. "When I miss a shot, I want to come back and take another one right away."

The Jayhawks hit 90 points for the second straight tournament game, the only time that's happen in the program's history.

Upstart Cal falls down
March 25, 1993

St. Louis - California wasn't supposed to be in the Sweet 16. But the Golden Bears upset defending national champion Duke in the second round. Guard Jason Kidd, who scored the winning basket against the Blue Devils and in the first-round victory over LSU was becoming a national sensation.

But Kidd never broke loose against the Jayhawks and counterpart Adonis Jordan. He finished with 13 points and 10 assists with most of his damage coming in the first half.

Cal took a 52-48 lead five minutes after halftime but Kansas used a 22-6 run to change the game. When the Golden Bears closed to single digits in the final three minutes, KU made 11 of its final 12 free throws to close the door.

"This team knows how to keep its poise," forward Richard Scott said.

The defensive work of forward Darrin Hancock was critical. He spent most of the second half on Lamond Murray. During the Jayhawks' big run, Murray missed four shots with Hancock in his face. In the second half, Murray missed 10 of 12 from the floor.

Rex Walters continued his hot shooting. He came into the game hitting 67 percent from the field and made eight of nine for most of his 24 points.

Indiana stood between Kansas and a Final Four berth, but before the Jayhawks cleared out of the locker room they had a visitor. Cal guard Jerod Haase wanted to offer more than his congratulations. He chatted with Walters about the program. Six weeks later, Haase announced he was transferring to Kansas.

On to the Final Four
March 27, 1993

St. Louis - North Carolina had done it at New Orleans during their national championship run of 1982, so Roy Williams, then a Tar Heel assistant, figured he'd give it a go at the Midwest Regional in St. Louis. The Jayhawks team bus stopped at the Mississippi River and everybody got out to spit.

It was the season for the ritual. Earlier in the year, Williams revealed that his jogging route in Lawrence took him by the cemetery where James Naismith is buried. Williams said he rubs the headstone for luck.

But spitting and rubbing didn't get the Jayhawks to the Final Four with a triumph over top-seeded Indiana. Kansas played perhaps its best game of the season to defeated the Hoosiers.

"This," Williams said, "is as good as it gets."

During the first 39 minutes, Kansas extended the lead to eight or nine five different times and Indiana overcame each deficit and briefly led three times. But Kansas was too good on this day. The Jayhawks shot 59.6 percent from the floor and got huge plays from just about everybody.

Kansas trailed 50-48 when Eric Pauley scored inside. Steve Woodberry then buried a three-pointer and Rex Walters added another. Calvin Rayford then stole the ball from Damon Bailey and drove for a layup and Indiana never quite recovered from the 10-0 run.

"Without question, Kansas was the better team today," Indiana coach Bobby Knight said.

Darrin Hancock, Woodberry and Richard Scott combined to hold national player of the year Calbert Cheaney to 22 points. He scored 36 in the Sweet 16 victory over Louisville. Cheaney did not score in the final 5:18 against the Jayhawks.

Rex Walters.

No Kidd-ing, Cal falls hard
Nov. 19, 1993

Lawrence - California wasn't the opening game of the 1993-94 season - both had to win Preseason NIT openers - but it may as well have been. The rematch of the 1993 Sweet 16 contest brought one of the most exciting players ever to Allen Field House, Jason Kidd.

Kidd had selected Cal over Kansas in a heated recruiting battle. The Golden Bears were ranked sixth; KU ninth. Besides Kidd, there was Lamond Murray. Both lived up to the hype by scoring 30 of Cal's 34 second-half points.

But Kansas took command early. At halftime, the Jayhawks led 41-22. Cal scored the first 10 points of the second half and closed to 46-41 with 13 minutes remaining.

A basket Murray didn't score changed the momentum. The margin was five when Murray went up for an 18-footer. But 5-7 point guard Calvin Rayford smacked it away from behind for the second blocked shot of his career. He converted two free throws to start a Kansas run.

Rayford had done some scouting and noticed something about Murray's shooting style while watching a tape of Cal defeat Santa Clara in the previous game.

"I saw that he takes the ball back on his shot," Rayford said. "I just waited on it and went after it."

The game was won in the front court. Forward Richard Scott finished with 20. "He was big-time for us," Williams said. "He stepped up."

So did center Greg Ostertag. He set a torrid early pace with seven rebounds, a block and steal in the first seven minutes.

Greg Ostertag blocks the shot of Monty Buckley.

On the night, Ostertag finished with 13 points and 12 rebounds.

Kansas had caught a break - Cal was playing without injured starters K.J. Roberts and Alfred Grigsby. But the Jayhawks also turned up the heat. They forced 19 turnovers, including seven by Kidd.

"We came in with two things to do," Cal coach Todd Bozeman said. "We had to play defense and rebound. In the first 20 minutes we didn't do either. And we needed to get scoring from somebody besides Kidd and Murray and we didn't get that."

The Jayhawks advanced to New York and defeated Minnesota and Massachusetts to capture their second NIT in four years. But neither triumph was as exhilarating as the quarterfinal against the Golden Bears.

Patrick Richey makes his way to the basket to score against a California defender.

Cal's Michael Stewart (foreground) and KU's Scot Pollard jostled for the ball.

Jayhawks prepare to take the floor before the 1993 contest with Indiana
that ended with Jacque Vaughn's game-winning three-pointer in overtime.

Vaughn beats buzzer, Hoosiers
Dec. 22, 1993

Lawrence - Jacque Vaughn came to Kansas as Roy Williams' most heralded recruit. In his 11th game, Vaughn proved why.

Vaughn swished a three-pointer from the right wing for the victory. The clock stopped at 0.2 seconds after the basket but the Hoosiers had no time to get off a final shot.

"Certain people are put here to do special things, and Jacque Vaughn is one of them," Williams said.

Some confusion in the offense forced Vaughn to be the hero. The first option was Steve Woodberry, who scored seven of his 13 in the overtime. But the screen that was supposed to set Woodberry free for a 12-footer broke down.

"I didn't think I could get it to Steve, so the best thing I could do was shoot the ball," Vaughn said. "I got a good release, a good arc and it went in."

The shot over Todd Leary ended a sensational overtime. Kansas scored on seven of eight possessions and Indiana on six of eight.

Lost in the celebration was the contribution of Sean Pearson. He nailed a three-pointer from the top of the key with 1:20 remaining to give the Jayhawks an 81-80 lead. When Indiana came up empty and KU answered with Woodberry's 12-footer the Jayhawks appeared home free.

But Damon Bailey threw in a three-point from deep on the left side to tie the score. Bailey was sensational, scoring 30 of his 36 after halftime. His two free throws with 25 seconds in regulation sent the game into overtime tied 70-70.

The final play was meant to go to Steve Woodberry.

The extra period hero was the other point guard, and when Vaughn's shot went through the net, he turned to the wild home crowd and smiled. Big time recruit. Big time shot.

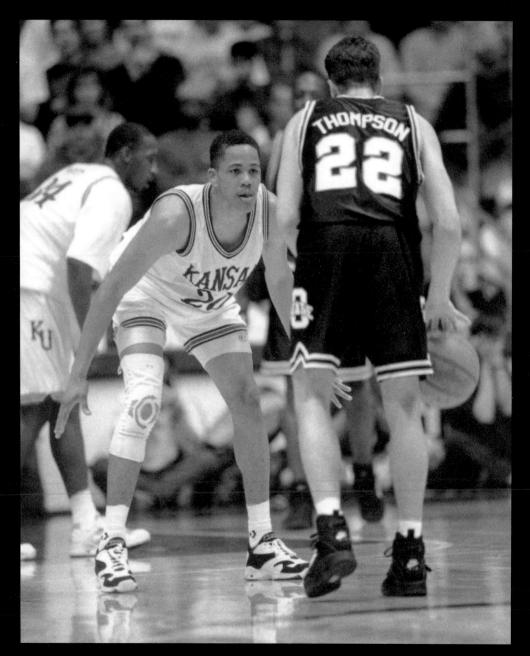

Steve Woodberry hawks Oklahoma State's Brooks Thompson
in a 1994 game won on Woodberry's buzzer beater.

Woodberry's shot clips Cowboys
Jan. 26, 1994

Lawrence - The only time in this decade that Kansas didn't win a conference championship was 1994. But that season produced two of the most dramatic victories under Roy Williams.

In December, Jacque Vaughn's three-pointer beat Indiana. A month later, Steve Woodberry provided the heroics.

The Jayhawks trailed 61-59 after the Cowboys' Fred Burley, a 77-percent free throw shooter made one free throw and missed the second. Oklahoma State's Terry Collins snared the rebound but lost it to Kansas center Greg Ostertag.

Ostertag dished to Vaughn, who hit Woodberry, streaking up the right sideline. Woodberry fired a three-pointer over Randy Rutherford and hit only net with 1.5 seconds remaining.

Woodberry, one of the top defenders to play for Williams, didn't celebrate. He immediately thought about defensive position and contested a 65-footer by Rutherford that banged off the backboard.

"I wanted to make sure we won or lost it on my shot," Woodberry said.

Woodberry had a chance to win the game in regulation, but his three-pointer missed with seven seconds remaining.

The winning shot marked the high moment for one of Williams' most unsung players. Woodberry, a star at Wichita South High, wasn't heavily recruited. He arrived at Kansas in time for the Jayhawks' 1991 Final Four run. He was good enough to start as a sophomore, but that's when transfer Rex Walters became eligible.

That meant two more years on the bench for Woodberry. During that span there was no better reserve in the Big Eight. In 1993, Woodberry was named second-team all-conference as a reserve.

Woodberry was a solid all-around player. Besides his defensive strength, Woodberry shot 42.3 percent on three-pointers and was a 79.1 percent free throw shooter. He averaged a team-best 15.5 points as a senior.

Woodberry worked quietly. He never said much to reporters after games. "You saw the game, what did you think?" was Woodberry's pet line. On this night his game was never louder.

Duncan, Deacons fall
March 19, 1994

Lexington, Ky. - You could see future greatness in Wake Forest freshman center Tim Duncan. But in the second-round of the NCAA Tournament, the Jayhawks had an answer, and it wasn't starting center Greg Ostertag.

Freshman Scot Pollard provided the critical basket. The Demon Deacons took their final lead at 49-48 with 9:07 remaining when Pollard tossed in a 7-foot jump hook over Duncan, who collected his fourth foul on the play.

The play started an 11-0 KU run. Pollard converted another three-point play and Jacque Vaughn gave the Jayhawks their first double-digit lead at 59-49 with a three-pointer from the left side.

After Duncan, who finished with 16 points, 15 rebounds and four blocked shots, got the fourth foul, Pollard and Vaughn combined for 14 of Kansas' next 16 points. Pollard finished with 13, Vaughn 12.

"With him able to step up like that when I'm not playing well is a real bonus to the team," Ostertag said.

According to Wake Forest star guard Randolph Childress, Vaughn also falls into that category.

"Steve Woodberry and Richard Scott get a lot of the credit, and I don't want to take anything away from them but they're good players," Childress said. "But Vaughn sets the tone for what Kansas is doing. He dictated the final minutes."

The Jayhawks' depth was a factor. After the Deacons took the 49-48 lead, they missed their next nine shots.

"It was us as much as it was Kansas," Wake coach Dave Odom said. "They played really well the entire 40 minutes, but they were outstanding in the final nine."

No. 1 Minutemen fall hard
Dec. 3, 1994

Anaheim, Calif. - A week before meeting the Jayhawks, Massachusetts routed top-ranked Arkansas. The Minutemen had a second chance to make a great impression at the John Wooden Classic.

Kansas had other ideas. The Jayhawks won by making big shots toward the end and afterwards made a strong case for being No. 1.

"We have to put this in perspective," guard Jacque Vaughn said. "We beat a No. 1 team but it's early. It does feel good, though."

Especially for Vaughn and other California-based Jayhawks. Vaughn, playing near his Pasadena home, finished with 14 points and 11 assists. Vaughn's biggest moments came in the final 90 seconds.

His two free throws restored a five-point advantage. He had been fouled 18 feet away from the basket with two seconds left on the shot clock.

Massachusetts forward Lou Roe answered with the last of his 33 points, making it 75-72. Vaughn struck again, not with a basket, but a drive. He sucked in the defense, dished to an open Jerod Haase on the wing. Haase buried the three-pointer with 31 seconds left.

Kansas had committed 14 turnovers in the first half and trailed 39-38. In the second half, the Jayhawks turned it over only three times. Massachusetts center Marcus Camby finished with two points in 28 minutes. He missed six of seven shots.

Playing in only his second college game, Raef LaFrentz had 18 points and nine rebounds.

But the KU backcourt was the difference. Vaughn and Haase combined for 30 points and 16 assists.

Kansas didn't make it to No. 1. The Jayhawks were ranked seventh before beating the Minutemen and fifth after.

Roy Williams on any opponent
"They aren't exactly St. Mary's Sisters of the Blind."

KU pounds Huskies
Jan. 28, 1995

Kansas City - This was a good time to be a Connecticut basketball fan. The men were ranked No. 2, the women were No. 1. Both were at Kemper Arena for a double-header.

The Huskies women won by 10 in one of their closest encounters of an undefeated season.

The men's game was an unexpected blowout. Connecticut entered the game as the nation's only unbeaten team at 15-0. It left with its worst defeat in three years.

From a 8-8 tie, the Jayhawks scored the next 10 and after Kansas made it 26-15, the margin never dipped into single digits.

"If you can't feel a game like this you aren't a player," guard Jacque Vaughn said. "The intensity, the emotion in the air. If you can't feel it you shouldn't be on the court."

Connecticut hardly was. Kansas missed seven shots and committed four turnovers in the final 4:30 of the first half and lost two points off its lead. The Huskies missed their first 11 three-point attempts.

"We played as poorly as we could play, I know that for a fact," Connecticut coach Jim Calhoun said.

The Jayhawks had been impressive in several non-conference victories. They have defeated No. 1 teams, captured regular-season tournaments. But this may have been the best under Roy Williams.

Kansas coaches and players had questioned the wisdom of a non-conference game well into the Big Eight season. Afterwards, it seemed like a great idea.

Jacque Vaughn

Big Country gets zero
March 5, 1995

Lawrence - If Kansas somehow could stop Oklahoma State's Bryant Reeves and Randy Rutherford, the Jayhawks liked their chances of winning the Big Eight championship on senior day and the regular season finale.

Kansas could do nothing with Rutherford, who bombed in 45 points and nailed 11 three-pointers. With anything at all from Reeves, the Cowboys would have won the title.

But Reeves, the former Big Eight player of the year, gave the Cowboys nothing. Zero. The only time in his college career - maybe his life - that Big Country was held scoreless.

"I would have bet a year's salary that he couldn't go 40 minutes without scoring," Oklahoma State coach Eddie Sutton said.

Reeves, who in the next month would lead the Cowboys to the Final Four and become a lottery pick in the NBA draft, missed 11 shots. He had scored 33 against the Jayhawks in the teams' previous meeting.

Rutherford scored 26 of the Cowboys' 34 second-half points. Greg Gurley, making the only start of his career, made two free throws with 10 minutes left to give the Jayhawks a seemingly comfortable 55-38 lead. But with Rutherford, Oklahoma State was never out of it.

"He embarrassed me," said Kansas guard Jerod Haase, one of several defenders who couldn't keep up.

Rutherford made three straight from behind the arc to make it 60-53 with six minutes remaining. But Gurley and Billy Thomas answered with three-pointers and the Jayhawks sprinted to the finish. Thomas made five of nine three-pointers for the game and finished with 17.

Rutherford's effort was the third best by a Kansas opponent and conjured memories of another season finale. Missouri's Anthony Peeler scored 43 in Lawrence in 1992. But as it did that day, Kansas prevailed and clipped nets that day.

"Rutherford was simply sensational," Roy Williams said. "I've always said one guy couldn't beat us, but he tried."

The league championship was No. 42 in Kansas' history.

"On days like this there's no better feeling in the world," Williams said. "You could put $10 million on the floor and give me a choice of that or the feelings I had today and there wouldn't be a choice."

Comeback marks first win over Bruins
Dec. 2, 1995

Lawrence - In one of the most anticipated games at Allen Field House, Kansas didn't arrive until the second half. In the opening 20 minutes, UCLA looked more like the team coming off the national championship rather than the one that had lost to Santa Clara earlier in the season.

After 17 minutes, the Bruins led 41-22. The halftime margin was 15. Embarrassing stuff for the nation's second ranked team that started three players - Jacque Vaughn, Paul Pierce and Scot Pollard - from Southern California.

"Maybe we wanted it too much," Roy Williams said. "We had Jacque and Jerod (Haase) on a fast break and I'm looking at the scoreboard because I know we're going to score, and the next thing I know Jacque's going into press row."

A defensive switch turned this game. Kansas went to a zone for a few minutes, and the Jayhawks were ignited. A 9-0 run closed the gap to 53-51. Moments later, Vaughn brought down the house by spinning around Cameron Dollar and Charles O'Bannon for a layup and a 54-53 lead.

The Jayhawks took the lead for good at 58-57 when Ryan Robertson scored inside.

"We could have won this game by 20 if we would've sustained our play in the second half," UCLA forward J.R. Henderson said.

Scot Pollard

Kansas was determined not to let that happen. Crushed on the boards on the first half, the Jayhawks outrebounded UCLA 26-10 after halftime.

But it was the zone that made the difference. Kansas was trailing 53-42 when it flashed a 2-3. The Bruins missed their next four shots and were shaken.

"That changed it up quite a bit," forward Raef LaFrentz said. "It put more pressure on their outside shooters and gave them a different look."

Vaughn and Pierce, both selected Kansas over UCLA, came on strong in the second half. Vaughn scored two points in the game's first 18 minutes and 20 after that. Pierce had 14 points and eight rebounds.

"I don't have to go back to L.A. and hear everybody's mouth," Pierce said. "So this was a must-win game."

Haase's shot sinks Arizona
March 22, 1996

Denver - Heroes abound for Kansas in its Sweet 16 victory over Arizona.

Jerod Haase's three-pointer from the right side with 39 seconds left provided the go-ahead points. It was his only basket of the second half.

"I just tried to relax," Haase said. "I knew it meant a lot, but I was able to focus at the task at hand."

Reserve forward B.J. Williams came up with the best game of his career with 18 points and nine rebounds. The Jayhawks needed his production. Starting forward Raef LaFrentz was held without a field goal for the first time in his career and finished with one point.

"B.J. was the big key to this game," Roy Williams said.

Point guard Jacque Vaughn kept it all together. It was his bounce pass that set up Haase's shot. Then, he buried two free throws to give KU an 83-79 lead.

It was a bizarre game. The Wildcats led by as many as 13 in the first half, but Kansas roared back behind Williams and Haase and led 41-39 at the break.

With seven minutes left, the Jayhawks led by 12. But Arizona went on a 17-2 run and twice held a three-point lead in the final two minutes.

With 1:02 remaining, Scot Pollard dropped in two free throws to cut the Wildcats lead to 79-78. Arizona's Reggie Geary missed a three-pointer and Haase chased down the long rebound. That set up the go-ahead possession.

The victory set up the West Regional final against Syracuse. Kansas went into the game having won six straight regional championship games. That streak came to an end when Vaughn's three-pointer to tie banged off the rim, preserving the Orangemen's 60-57 victory.

Jerod Haase

1996-97 Men's Basketball Team

A Century of Jayhawk Triumphs

Kansas 72, Cincinnati 65

Jayhawks stare down Bearcats
Dec. 4, 1996

Chicago - Ah, technology. No more than 15 minutes after top-ranked Kansas had defeated fourth-ranked Cincinnati in the Great Eight forward Paul Pierce was watching highlights of his remarkable second half in the Jayhawks locker room - the one usually occupied by the home standing Chicago Bulls.

Pierce nails a three. Cheers.

Pierce flies through the lane for a slam. Louder cheers.

"I made up my mind that I could do more things to help the team than what I was doing in the first half," Pierce said.

Pierce sparked an against-the-odds second-half comeback with outstanding all-around play. He scored 15 of his 17 after the break on a variety of shots, a three-pointer that gave Kansas its first lead of the half, a slam off an inbounds pass that energized the Jayhawks, then a combination of both.

Pierce pulled up to fire a trey, then saw a sliver of an opening to the basket. Pump fake, dribble, drive, slam, hang. United Center patrons witness such moves on a regular basis from prized tenant, Michael Jordan. Artful individual moves are rare for the Jayhawks.

But that's what Pierce provides, maybe more so than any Kansas player since Danny Manning. When the moment calls for superb athleticism, crafting a play when defense takes away what systematic passing and cutting, Pierce can deliver.

The comeback spark was a third foul on Cincinnati's powerful forward Danny Fortson. He collected the foul with 18 minutes, 35 seconds to play and went to the bench after his 18th point put the Bearcats ahead 37-23.

But with Fortson watching from the bench, KU started an 18-2 blitz, the run starting with every starter scoring a basket. When Billy Thomas and Pierce finished the run by swishing three-pointers, Kansas had its first lead since the opening minutes, 41-39.

Fortson returned and was just as rugged. But the game's tone had changed completely. Kansas didn't stop scoring. Another 12-3 run gave KU a 55-46 lead.

After that, Cincinnati didn't get closer than five. A Darnell Burton three-point attempt that would have cut the margin to four with two minutes to play spun out, ending the Bearcats' last gasp.

Kansas had won the Maui Classic, but defeating the Bearcats was the most important non-conference triumph. Cincinnati had lost its preseason No. 1 ranking by falling to Xavier but not its mystique. The Jayhawks were intimidated early.

But in the end, Kansas made a resounding statement in its first test as the nation's No. 1-ranked team.

Streak over Bruins grows
Dec. 7, 1996

Los Angeles - Kansas never had much luck with UCLA. Some of the best KU teams - 1966, 1971, 1978 - ran into a Bruins team that was a little better.

But in 1996-97, the Jayhawks clearly were better. They had just assumed the No. 1 ranking and the 17th-ranked Bruins were still recovering from the stunning coaching change. Jim Harrick had been fired before the season and assistant Steve Lavin was named his successor.

When Kansas and UCLA met in Pauley Pavillion for the first time since 1965, the Bruins were in disarray and the Jayhawks took full advantage. KU led by as many as 28 in the first half.

A six-minute stretch in the first half may have been the Jayhawks' best during the season. Raef LaFrentz scored eight straight, on his way to 31. The Bruins couldn't protect the ball and wound up with 18 first-half turnovers. In the stretch, Kansas outscored UCLA 30-6.

Just so Roy Williams would have something to talk about in the lock-

Paul Pierce

erroom, UCLA scored the final seven points of the half.

If it wasn't LaFrentz finishing inside, it was Billy Thomas pulling up to bury a three-pointer. He hit all three of his attempts in the first half and finished with 18 points.

For the California-born Jayhawks it was an especially satisfying day. Jacque Vaughn, Paul Pierce, Scot Pollard and Jerod Haase all reveled in the triumph, although Vaughn couldn't play because of an injured wrist.

Haase has only known success in Pauley. As a freshman at Cal, Haase scored 16 points and had five assists in a victory over the Bruins. The game was played one day after the unexpected death of his father, Gary.

After losing the first eight games in the series, Kansas had now defeated UCLA twice.

"It's tremendous," Pollard said. "A lot of people probably didn't think we'd do it. Maybe some of us didn't think we could do it."

Kansas did it. Resoundingly.

Down 16, KU roars back
Jan. 29, 1997

Lubbock, Tex. - Game No. 2 without injured starting Scot Pollard looked like a lost cause. Kansas was at Texas Tech, a team coming off a crushing loss at Iowa State and sky high for the visit from the top-ranked Jayhawks.

The most inspired Red Raider was center Tony Battie, who had scored only three against the Cyclones. Battie scored the game's first two baskets and was on his way to a 29-point, 10-rebound game.

For a half, Battie and Tech seemed unbeatable. The Red Raiders roared to a 16-point lead and led 47-33 at halftime.

"In the first half, we were just sorry," Roy Williams said. "I was as mad as I've ever been with this group."

So much so that during the final media timeout of the first half, with stuffed Lubbock Municipal Coliseum going crazy as Battie was dunking every way possible on the Jayhawks, Williams stepped out of the huddle and let assistant Matt Doherty do the talking, or chewing out.

"I told them, I wasn't talking to their butts," Williams said.

Halftime wasn't much friendlier. But the Jayhawks got the message. Tech had shot 54 percent from the field in the first half. Kansas made the adjustments.

Early in the second half guards Jerod Haase and Ryan Robertson came up with four straight steals that sparked a 14-2 run that gave Kansas the lead. Tech missed 21 of 33 field goals in the second half. Guard Cory Carr, the Big 12's second leading scorer, hurt the Red Raiders with his cold shooting (six for 21) and finished with 16.

Even Battie, so strong for so long, faltered down the stretch. He missed the front end of two bonus opportunities that allowed Kansas to keep a distance.

As for board work, KU pulled down 15 offensive rebounds in the second half. Reserve front-liner T.J. Pugh, in a career high 19 minutes, yanked down nine rebounds, also a personal best.

"We knew we could play better," Pugh said. "I thought we were lacking intensity in the first half. That's what we tried to change."

The triumph made Kansas 21-0, and was even more impressive than the one a few days earlier at Colorado. The Buffaloes had nobody inside to take advantage of Pollard's absence. In Battie, Tech had one of the nation's best centers.

But with all the advantages - Battie, a hostile crowd, motivation from a previous poor performance, a fast start - Tech couldn't win and talk of an undefeated Kansas started to surface.

"It's hard to say a team can go undefeated," guard Ryan Robertson said. "It's hard to imagine, but as long as we take it game by game, as long as we do that, we have a chance to win every game. I definitely think it's in our grasp."

Emotions overflow on Senior Day
Feb. 22, 1997

Lawrence - Nobody does senior day like Kansas.

Allen Field House was jammed a hour before the home finale against Kansas State. Senior days are always emotional, but this occasion was exceptional because of this class.

To coach Roy Williams, the scholarship class of Jacque Vaughn, Scot Pollard, Jerod Haase and B.J. Williams embodied what's good in college basketball.

"They've made me feel what good hands this place is in because of the kind of kids they are," Williams said. "When you talk about our seniors, I could put any one of them at my house and say 'Take care of my kids, I'll be back in four days,' and I wouldn't worry the slightest bit. I've got the best

group of kids in America. Other coaches can say it. But no coach can say it with the conviction Roy Williams does."

In each of the last four years for at least a week, KU has been ranked No. 1. Regular seasons have been more satisfying than postseasons. This class never played in a Final Four, and became the first class under Williams not to do so.

But that didn't diminish the feelings Roy Williams held for this class, and it showed on senior day against Kansas State. During the senior introductions, roses and carnations flooded the floor. When it came time for the starters to walk on the floor, Williams sent seven: the four scholarship seniors, junior Raef LaFrentz and two walk-on seniors Joel Branstrom and Steve Ransom.

Jerod Haase and Scot Pollard on Senior Day.

Jacque Vaughn gets a hug from his mother.

The walk-ons stood in the Wildcats' backcourt, ready to take the tip, until referee Tom Harrington walked over to the Kansas bench and wanted to know if coach Williams planned to follow through, which, had Harrington stepped into the center circle for the jump, he would have called a technical foul. Williams then beckoned the walk-ons off the floor.

"This was as emotional a day there's been since I've been here and it got so emotional it became a distraction," Williams said.

Scot Pollard and Roy Williams after the victory.

Which explains why Kansas State led 31-30 at halftime, and even that was emotional as the jersey of one of the school's greatest athletes, Ray Evans, was retired. But the Jayhawks didn't ruin the day with a loss. Kansas seized control in the opening minutes after the break when LaFrentz picked up the pace. His two free throws with 16 minutes, 5 seconds remaining gave Kansas the lead for good at 39-38.

A late burst allowed Williams to substitute freely at the game's end to maximize crowd response. Pollard, playing for the first time since his foot fracture, offered a farewell salute by swishing a three-pointer on his first attempt – career shot No. 731 – with 2:56 remaining.

"I'll never take another one in college," Pollard said. "I wanted to go in the record book as the only Kansas player to make the only three-pointer he ever attempted."

Then, while K-State's Manny Dies stood at the free-throw line, the procession of replacements began. Haase, then Williams, then Vaughn were replaced for the final time at home. Branstrom and Ransom were inserted. Each scored a basket before they were replaced.

Oh yeah, the victory clinched the Big 12 championship for Kansas.

After the game and the net-cutting ceremony, seniors gave speeches. Pollard did a cartwheel, Haase called Williams a "father-like" figure, Vaughn choked up as he hugged his coach.

There will always be a senior day at Kansas. But the emotion on this day may never be matched.

March 1, 1989
Kansas 80, Nebraska 71

F Mark Randall	JR
F Lincoln Minor	SR
F Sean Alvarado	SR
G Milt Newton	SR
G Scooter Barry	SR

March 3, 1990
Kansas 96, Iowa State 63

F Mark Randall	JR
F Rick Calloway	SR
C Freeman West	SR*
G Kevin Pritchard	SR
G Jeff Gueldner	SR

Feb. 26, 1991
Kansas 88, Iowa State 57

F Kirk Wagner	SR*
F Mike Maddox	SR
C Mark Randall	SR
G Terry Brown	SR
G Adonis Jordan	SO

March 3, 1992
Kansas 97, Missouri 89

F Alonzo Jamison	SR
F Malcom Nash	SR
C David Johanning	SR*
G Lane Czaplinski	SR*
G Rex Walters	JR

March 3, 1993
Kansas 94, Nebraska 83

F Darrin Hancock	JR
F Richard Scott	JR
C Eric Pauley	SR
G Rex Walters	SR
G Adonis Jordan	SR

March 3, 1994
Kansas 97, Iowa State 79

F Patrick Richey	SR
F Blake Weichbrodt	SR*
C Richard Scott	SR
G Jacque Vaughn	FR
G Steve Woodberry	SR

March 5, 1995
Kansas 78, Oklahoma State 62

F Raef LaFrentz	FR
F Greg Gurley	SR*
C Greg Ostertag	SR
G Jacque Vaughn	SO
G Scott Novosel	SR*

Feb. 26, 1996
Kansas 87, Missouri 65

F T.J. Whatley	SR*
F Sean Pearson	SR
C Raef LaFrentz	SO
G Calvin Rayford	SR
G Jacque Vaughn	JR

Feb. 22, 1997
Kansas 78, Kansas State 58

F B.J. Williams	SR
F Raef LaFrentz	JR
C Scot Pollard	SR
G Jerod Haase	SR
G Jacque Vaughn	SR

* career first start

Senior Day

"It seems like we're always down there for that damn Senior Day," *former Iowa State coach Johnny Orr.*

No team in the nation makes a bigger deal of Senior Day than Kansas. Scholarship seniors start. No exception.

Conference membership is like a family, forever growing, always changing. A constant throughout the century has been Kansas' basketball superiority.

From the Missouri Valley Intercollegiate Athletic Association to the Big Six, Big Seven, Big Eight and Big 12, the Jayhawks have captured titles under all banners.

League affiliation started in 1907. Schools had loosely followed rules of the Western Conference, later known as the Big Ten, set out on their own. On Jan. 12 in Kansas City, representatives from Kansas, Missouri, Nebraska, Iowa and Washington University of St. Louis formed the Missouri Intercollegiate Athletic Association.

The first year of competition was 1907-08. Nebraska and Iowa were the league's first football champions with 1-0 records. In basketball, Kansas swept all league games against Missouri and Nebraska under coach Phog Allen, to win the first basketball championship with a 6-0 record.

The conference quickly grew. Drake and Ames College, later known as Iowa State, joined in 1908. Iowa left in 1911, but Kansas State joined in 1913. Grinnell's brief period as a league member started in 1919. Oklahoma joined in 1920 and Oklahoma A&M in 1925.

The league changed direction in 1928. As interest in college athletics grew, schools with greater emphasis in sports sought more autonomy in decision making. Grinnell, Drake, Washington and Oklahoma A&M were out. The survivors - Kansas, Kansas State, Missouri, Nebraska, Oklahoma and Iowa State - unofficially became known as the Big Six.

Colorado joined in 1947 to make it the Big Seven, and Allen's friendship with Oklahoma A&M coach Hank Iba paved the way for the Aggies' return to the fold in 1957, when the school officially changed its name to Oklahoma State. The first year of Big Eight basketball was 1958-59.

The next 3 1/2 decades provided unusual stability. While other leagues positioned themselves for football television and basketball tournament dollars, the Big Eight stood with a pat hand. But with leagues like the Southeastern, Big Ten and Atlantic Coast adding members change was inevitable in the Big Eight.

With the breakup of the Southwest Conference, the formation of the Big 12 was announced in 1994. Baylor, Texas, Texas A&M and Texas Tech joined the Big Eight schools for the 1996-97 season.

The first basketball championship, just as the first Missouri Valley title, went to the Jayhawks.

Conference affiliation timeline

	MVIAA	Big 6	Big 7	Big 8	Big 12
Kansas		1907			
Missouri		1907			
Nebraska		1907			
Iowa	1907	1911			
Washington, Mo.	1907	1928			
Ames (Iowa St.)	1908				
Drake	1908	1928			
Kansas State		1913			
Grinnell		1919	1928		
Oklahoma		1920			
Oklahoma A&M		1925-28		1958	
Colorado			1947		
Baylor					1996
Texas					1996
Texas A&M					1996
Texas Tech					1996

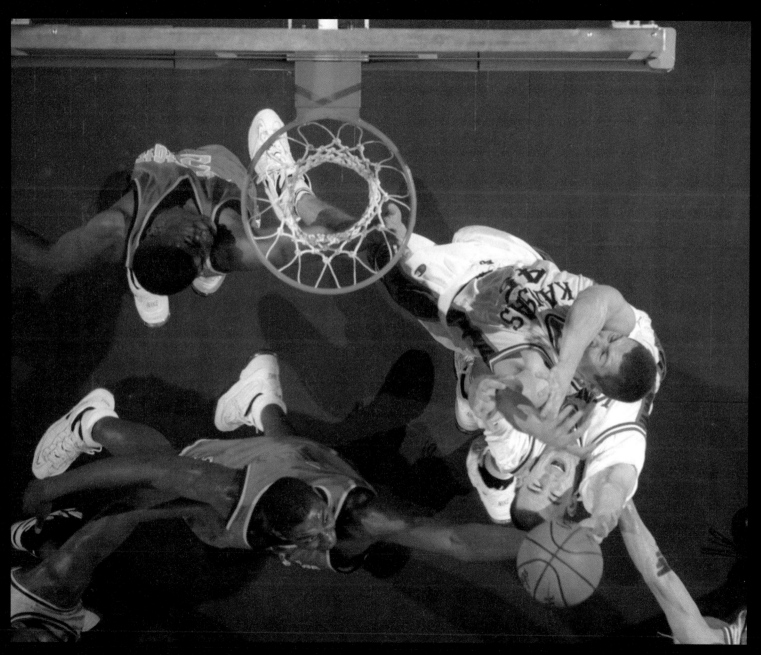

Raef LaFrentz and T. J. Pugh battle with Iowa State's Kelvin Cato in the Big 12 Tournament semifinal game.

T. J. Pugh and Paul Pierce surround Iowa State's Kelvin Cato.

New nemesis falls hard
March 7, 1997

Kansas City - Since Tim Floyd arrived at Iowa State in 1995, Kansas played the Cyclones more times than any other conference opponent. And most games were nail-biters.

In 1995, Fred Hoiberg scored the Cyclones' final 17 points to lead a comeback victory in Ames. The next year, Iowa State defeated Kansas by a point for its first conference tournament title.

The Jayhawks had won both regular-season battles in 1997, but the third game was set for Kemper, where the Cyclones had won the previous two encounters.

The third straight tournament meeting was this semifinal, and Iowa State couldn't have drawn up a better defensive strategy. For the first time in five years (149 games), Kansas didn't make a three-point shot. Missed all eight, including two airballs.

Unfortunately for Iowa State, the Jayhawks played better defense. "That was as well as we've been guarded since I've been at Iowa State," said Floyd.

The Cyclones took 50 shots and missed 35. Guard Dedric Willoughby, who lit up the Jayhawks for 36 in their past meeting, was harassed, mostly by Jerod Haase, into a three for 13 performance and 10 points.

Willoughby made two three-pointers in the game's first 10 minutes, and his only field goal after that came on a breakaway slam set up when Kansas center Scot Pollard threw away a pass.

"It was clear they wanted this game bad because the defense they played," Iowa State center Kelvin Cato said.

There may have been another motivation. Kansas got word it wasn't as good a defensive team as the Cyclones. "We heard a quote from one of their players that our defense was pretty good but theirs was great," guard Billy Thomas said. "We wanted to prove that we had the best defense in the league. Today, I think that showed."

The effort was strong throughout but never more effective than in the first 10 minutes of the second half. Kansas led 27-23 at the break. The Cyclones opened the second half with an air ball by Willoughby, a turnover, then two free throws from Kenny Pratt. Nearly 10 minutes and 16 possessions passed before the Cyclones got another field goal.

In the stretch, Iowa State missed 10 shots and committed seven turnovers. Cato was constantly having the ball slapped away. Willoughby never got the ball in a position to shoot because the Jayhawks double-teamed him whenever they could.

"I never got a chance to get my feet set on any shot I had," Willoughby said. "It's the best defense I've seen since I've been at ISU."

His bench demeanor is usually serious, but Roy Williams shares a smile with Paul Pierce as the Jayhawks put the finishing touches on a Big 12 Tournament victory. Pierce was named the event's MVP.

KU first Big 12 tourney champ
March 8, 1997

Kansas City - Kansas and Missouri hadn't met in the league tournament for a decade. Roy Williams and Norm Stewart had never clashed at Kemper Arena. The way the Jayhawks handled the Tigers in the championship game of the inaugural Big 12 Tournament, perhaps the schools should wait another 10 years before a rematch.

Kansas improved to 32-1 and rolled into the NCAA Tournament with a victory that would have ranked as the most decisive in the 20 years of the Big Eight event. Of course, this was the Big 12. It felt good, anyway.

"It should be fun walking into class today," Kansas point guard Jacque Vaughn said.

Four games in four days had worn out 10th seeded Missouri, 16-17. They staggered off the floor at halftime having made only nine of 28 from the floor. Derek Grimm opened the Tigers' scoring with a three-pointer that gave Missouri its only lead of the day at 3-2. After that, the Tigers missed nine of their next 10 from behind the arc.

Kansas caught fire in the final nine minutes of the first half and put it away. The score was 24-17 when Raef LaFrentz dropped in a 10-footer.

Jacque Vaughn found a cutting Paul Pierce, who attacked the basket with a vicious slam for a three-point play. Two more Missouri free throws, then six unanswered Kansas points. A three-point play by the Tigers' Kelly Thames, then 14 straight by the Jayhawks.

Pierce hit from everywhere, finished with 30 and was named the tournament's most valuable player. "It was just one of those days," Pierce said. "I was definitely feeling it, and my teammates recognized that."

So much so Pierce was starting to get on center Scot Pollard's nerves. "I told him, 'Could you miss some shots so I could get some rebounds?' " Pollard said.

The game was especially satisfying for Pierce. In the Jayhawks' lone loss this season, in double-overtime at Missouri, he fouled out after scoring two points.

Vaughn felt good, too. The Jayhawks had won their third straight league title in 1997 but this was the first tournament championship for the senior class.

"Four years for me, and now a tournament championship," Vaughn said. "It's definitely special."

Williams on getting
Kansas a national championship

66 We've been knocking at the door and we're going to keep knocking until we've knocked it down. **99**

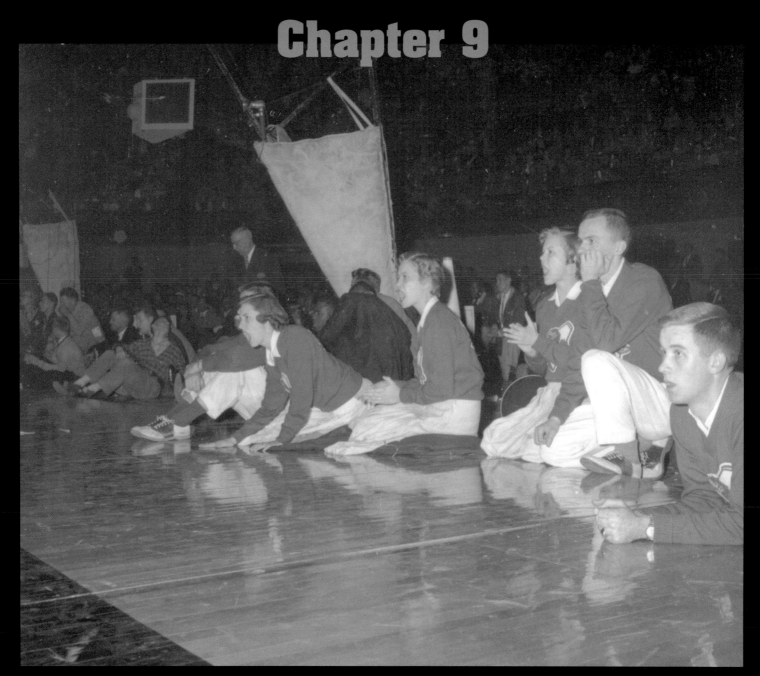

Chapter 9

The Top 10 Victories

Ranking 100 victories is impossible. Who's to say a 1992 victory over Missouri was greater than a 1943 triumph over Oklahoma? But 10 seems a workable number. The top 10 victories in order:

1. Kansas 83, Oklahoma 79, 1988. The NCAA championship gave college basketball its greatest half and one of its greatest upsets.

2. Kansas 80, St. John's 63, 1952. This NCAA championship elevated the status of Phog Allen, Clyde Lovellette and the Kansas tradition. Without it, KU would have fewer NCAA titles than San Francisco and North Carolina State.

3. Kansas 71, Kansas State 58, 1988. The Midwest Regional championship, which drew more than 31,000 at the Silverdome, provided the highest stakes in the 250 meetings between the Sunflower rivals.

4. Kansas 23, Missouri 20, 1923. Phog Allen was so frustrated losing to the Tigers he told his wife he'd quit if KU couldn't beat Missouri in Columbia and win an outright Big Six title. Allen told many tall tales, and we'll never know how serious he was, but this was a huge victory and gave Kansas its second straight Helms Foundation national championship.

5. Kansas 87, Northwestern 69, 1957. With 52 points and 31 rebounds, Wilt Chamberlain's debut was more than advertised. Suddenly, Allen Field House, the second largest on-campus facility when it debuted two years earlier, wasn't big enough.

6. Kansas 150, Kentucky 95, 1989. The most points by a Kansas team and the most allowed by Kentucky.

7. Kansas 43, Southern Cal 42, 1940. The Jayhawks weren't favored to win the Big Six, much less reach the Western Regional title game. The Trojans had the nation's second best team but Howard Engleman's basket sent KU to the championship game at Kansas City.

8. Kansas 93, Arkansas 81, 1991. The powerful Razorbacks were thought to be the only team with a chance to beat UNLV. In the Southeast Regional title game at Charlotte, the Jayhawks outscored Arkansas by 24 in the second half to reach the Final Four.

9. Kansas 83, Indiana 77, 1993. The Hoosiers were ranked first, but the Kansas victory in the Midwest Regional championship game at St. Louis prevented the only Final Four in history with four No. 1 seeds.

10. Kansas 26, Missouri 16, 1922. The Tigers had already defeated Kansas in Lawrence and were rolling toward their third straight outright Big Six title. The Jayhawks victory in Columbia prevented that streak and started one of six straight league titles for Kansas. It's also the game the Helms Foundation used to declare KU the national champion that year.

Kansas standout losses.

Feb. 3, 1899
Kansas City YMCA 16, Kansas 5

Kansas City -
Such an inglorious beginning. OK, nobody shed tears after the first game in Kansas history. But a record endures from the opener. The five points is the fewest in the history of the program.

March 28, 1936
Utah State 50, Kansas 31

Lawrence -
Phog Allen had done more than anyone to have basketball included in the Olympic Games. But he lost his chance to reach the Olympic play-off finals in New York by losing the deciding game of a best-of-three to the unheralded Aggies.

March 18, 1953
Indiana 69, Kansas 68

Kansas City -
The Jayhawks bid to become the second team to win successive championships (Oklahoma A&M won in 1946 and 1947) died in the final seconds. Guard Allen Kelley was supposed to take the final shot but was closely guarded. Instead, Jerry Alberts' shot skipped across the rim and the Hoosiers beat KU for a national title for the second time.

March 23, 1957
North Carolina 54, Kansas 53, three overtimes

Kansas City -
The Tar Heels were supposed to be exhausted after a triple-overtime victory over Michigan State in the semifinals the day before. But when the Jayhawks got a lead in the second half, they pulled it out. North Carolina caught its breath and Kansas.

March 12, 1966
Texas Western 81, Kansas 80, two overtimes

Lubbock, Tex. -
Guard Jo Jo White could have sat out the entire year and started his eligibility the next season. Ted Owens inserted him midway through the 1965-66 season because he thought the Jayhawks could go a long way. They would have been in the Final Four had White not been ruled to have stepped out of bounds just before a game-winning shot.

March 20, 1981
Wichita State 66, Kansas 65

New Orleans - Darnell Valentine missed a layup with 20 seconds to play that would have given Kansas a three-point lead in the Battle of New Orleans. Had he not taken the shot, Wichita State would have been forced to foul. The teams hadn't played since 1955, and this one was ever-so-sweet for the Shockers.

March 29, 1986
Duke 71, Kansas 67

Dallas - The Blue Devils were ranked first and had already defeated the Jayhawks during the regular season. But Duke was a fading team and Kansas knew it had a great chance of getting to the title game. Danny Manning's early foul trouble and an injury that forced Archie Marshall from the game killed the Jayhawks.

March 22, 1992
Texas-El Paso 66, Kansas 60

Dayton, Ohio - After the Jayhawks disposed of Howard in the first round, the players watched another first-round game, a poorly played contest between Evansville and Texas-El Paso. Top-seeded Kansas couldn't have been impressed. They were after playing the ninth-seeded Miners, who spoiled Kansas' chance of playing the Midwest Regional at Kansas City.

March 24, 1996
Syracuse 60, Kansas 57

Denver - A year earlier, Kansas had its worst shooting game of the season in a tournament loss to Virginia. The second-seeded Jayhawks repeated the performance against the fourth-seeded Orangemen, KU went four for 25 on three-pointers. The final miss was Jacque Vaughn's trey to tie it just before the buzzer.

March 21, 1997
Arizona 85, Kansas 82

Birmingham, Ala. - It was of no consolation that the Wildcats went on to beat North Carolina and Kentucky to win the championship. Kansas trailed throughout the second half. A furious rally, from 13 down in the final three minutes, got Kansas to 2. But three chances from behind the arc fell short, sealing KU's doom.

Jayhawks in the Final Four

1940
Municipal Auditorium, Kansas City
semifinal   Kansas 43, Southern Cal 42
championship Indiana 60, Kansas 42

NOTES: Three Jayhawks made all-Big Six: Bob Allen, Howard Engleman and Ralph Miller, who led the team in scoring at 9.1. Nobody who played for the 1939-40 team ranks in the top 35 in KU career scoring...There was no Final Four the way we know it today. Kansas emerged from the Western Regional final in Kansas City and Indiana from the Eastern final in Indianapolis...The ``Hurryin Hoosiers" blitzed to a 32-19 halftime lead and coasted in the second half. Senior forward Marvin Huffman was named MVP of the finals. He averaged 4.3 points during the season and had 12 in the title game...The all-tournament team included Huffman, Indiana's Jay McCreary and Bill Menke and the Jayhawks' Bob Allen and Howard Engleman.

1952
Edmundson Pavilion, Seattle
semifinal   Kansas 74, Santa Clara 55
championship Kansas 80, St. John's 63

NOTES: For the first time, four regional finalists met at one site, creating a Final Four. Upsets ruled the tournament. St. John's knocked off top-ranked Kentucky then No. 2 Illinois. Unranked Santa Clara defeated UCLA and Wyoming, both in the polls...Everybody who suited up played for Kansas...Lovellette led the all-Final Four team which also included teammate Dean Kelley, Bob Zawoluk and Ron MacGilvary of St. John's and Illinois' John Kerr.

1953
Municipal Auditorium, Kansas City
semifinal   Kansas 79, Washington 53
championship Indiana 69, Kansas 68

NOTES: B.H. Born averaged 1.7 points as Lovellette's backup the previous year. He led KU with an 18.9 average as a junior and matched that figure in 1954, his senior season...Born was the center of controversy in the title game when officials ruled he had collected his fourth foul near the end of the third quarter. Members on press row had Born for four, and after consulting with the scorer's table, the official changed allowed Born to stay. Indiana coach Branch McCracken went nuts but had the final laugh... Born was the tournament MVP, which is why his jersey is retired at Allen Field House. Also on the Final Four honor team: KU's Dean Kelley, Indiana's Bob Leonard and Don Schlundt and Washington's Bob Houbregs.

1957
Municipal Auditorium, Kansas City
semifinal   Kansas 80, San Francisco 56
championship North Carolina 54, Kansas 53, 3 overtimes

NOTES: Tar Heels coach Frank McGuire, who lost to the Jayhawks as the St. John's coach five years earlier got revenge. McGuire sent 5-10 Tommy Kearns out to jump center against 7-1 Wilt Chamberlain. Writers said McGuire was trying to confuse the Jayhawks, but he later said there really was no strategy to the move...Carolina led 29-22 at halftime. Regulation ended 46-46, the first overtime 48-48 and the second overtime 48-48. KU led 53-52 when North Carolina's Joe Quigg scoring the winning hoop with six seconds left. All-Final Four: Chamberlain, the Tar Heels' Lenny Rosenbluth and Pete Brennan, Michigan State's John Green and Gene Brown of San Francisco.

1971
Astrodome, Houston
semifinal   UCLA 68, Kansas, 60
consolation Western Kentucky 77, Kansas 75

NOTES: The eight-point loss to the Bruins was one of UCLA's closest Final Four victories. UCLA center Steve Patterson credited his dominating title game effort, 29 points and eight rebounds against Villanova, to his poor performance against KU (six points) ...Four Kansas starters went on to play in the NBA or ABA: Dave Robisch, Bud Stallworth, Roger Brown and Pierre Russell...No Kansas player made the all-Final Four team.

1974
Greensboro Coliseum, Greensboro, N.C.
semifinal   Marquette 64, Kansas 51
consolation   UCLA 78, Kansas 61

NOTES: Before the third-place game, coach Ted Owens heard that Bill Walton and other UCLA starters had no interest in playing against Kansas. Owens went to the Bruins locker room and asked the starters to play. They did, and UCLA won easily...Norm Cook became the first freshman to start all games for Kansas. Freshmen became eligibile for varsity play a year earlier ... No Jayhawk made the all-Final Four team.

1986
Reunion Arena, Dallas
semifinal   Duke 71, Kansas 67

NOTES: The consolation game was done away with after 1981, which was just as well because Kansas couldn't win them anyway...Danny Manning and Ron Kellogg made all-Big Eight, Manning won the first of three straight league MVPs...During the regular season, Kansas lost at Iowa State. Larry Brown or Danny Manning never won a game at Ames, Iowa...In the final year before the three-point shot, the 1985-86 Jayhawks shot a school record 55.6 percent from the floor.

1988
Kemper Arena, Kansas City
semifinal   Kansas 66, Duke 59
championship   Kansas 83, Oklahoma 79

NOTES: Opponents shot 50.9 percent against KU for the season, the highest in school history...Over a month-long period at mid-season, the Jayhawks only victory came over Division II Hampton...Larry Brown became the first coach to leave for another job after winning the NCAA championship, and Kansas is the only team not permitted to defend its title because of probation...Final Four MVP Manning joined teammate Milt Newton and Oklahoma's Stacey King and Dave Sieger with Arizona's Sean Elliott on the honor team.

1991
Hoosier Dome, Indianapolis
semifinal   Kansas 79, North Carolina 73
championship   Duke 72, Kansas 65

NOTES: Forward Mike Maddox lost his chance to become the first Kansas player and the first in college basketball since the UCLA teams to own two championship rings...Roy Williams said he was perturbed when Jayhawks fans cheered for Duke against Nevada-Las Vegas in the other semifinal. He thought KU had a better shot against the Runnin' Rebels...Regional MVP Alonzo Jamison went 1 for 10 from the field against Duke...Mark Randall joined Duke's Christian Laettner (MVP), Bobby Hurley and Bill McCaffrey and UNLV's Anderson Hunt on the all-Final Four team.

1993
Superdome, New Orleans
semifinal   North Carolina 78, Kansas 68

NOTES: Three-point shooting sparked the Jayhawks' tournament run. Rex Walters made all six against Ball State. Even the loss to the Tar Heels, KU made 11 of 20 from behind the arc...Future NBA players on the team included Walters, Greg Ostertag, Darrin Hancock and even Adonis Jordan played a few games...Ben Davis is in the 1992-93 team picture but transferred before the season started.

All-time teams

All-James Naismith/Phog Allen I (1898-1909)

George McCune
Phog Allen
William Miller
Earl Woodward
Tommy Johnson

All-William Hamilton (1909-1919)

Lefty Sproull
Dutch Lonborg
Red Brown
Vern Long
John Bunn

All-Phog Allen II (1919-1956)
1919-1938

Paul Endacott
Tusten Ackerman
William Johnson
Fred Pralle
Charlie T. Black
Sixth man: Ted O'Leary

1939-1956

Clyde Lovellette
Howard Engleman
Charlie B. Black
Ray Evans
B.H. Born
Sixth man: Otto Schnellbacher

All-Dick Harp (1956-1964)

Bill Bridges
Wilt Chamberlain
Nolen Ellison
Jerry Gardner
Wayne Hightower
Sixth man: George Unseld

All-Ted Owens (1964-1983)

Dave Robisch
Bud Stallworth
Darnell Valentine
Walt Wesley
JoJo White
Sixth man: Norm Cook

All-Larry Brown (1983-1988)

Cedric Hunter
Ron Kellogg
Danny Manning
Kevin Pritchard
Calvin Thompson
Sixth man: Greg Dreiling

All-Roy Williams (1988-1997)

Raef LaFrentz
Paul Pierce
Mark Randall
Jacque Vaughn
Rex Walters
Sixth man: Steve Woodberry

Danny Manning is mobbed by fans and teammates after he led his team to victory over the Oklahoma Sooners in the 1988 national championship.

Credits